ANDREWMARTIN

Interior Design Review Volume 17

teNeues

One of the hallmarks of great designers is the ability to subjugate their egos and let their work play second fiddle to the superior claim of other elements. Sometimes, the architecture may be so splendid that decoration must be pared right back. This year's wonderful winner of the Andrew Martin Interior Design Award, Rose Uniacke, gives a masterclass in how her austere restraint underpins the haunting beauty of her rooms.

Sometimes it may be that the surrounding views are so overwhelming that the emphasis of the interior should be heavily calibrated towards the exterior. The simplicity of Stefano Dorata's style allows the majesty of nature to be the star. Art collections put a particular responsibility on the designer. Pope Benedict said 'art is like an open doorway to the infinite and a truth that goes beyond everyday reality.' In 2000 years, no pontiff ever said that about a cushion. Pope Benedict then told a group of artists that included Anish Kapoor and Zahad Hadid 'you are to be heralds and witness of hope and humanity'. So woe betide the interior designers who get in the way.

All the great religions have harnessed the power of art. Pope Benedict's predecessor, Nicholas V (1397-1455) declared that 'the mission of art was for the greater authority of the Roman church'. In recent years, attitudes have changed. The line between art and consumerism has become blurred. As early as the 1950's, Richard Hamilton was writing that art should be 'popular, transient, expendable, low cost, mass produced, young, witty, sexy, gimmicky, glamorous and big business'. None can deny that pop art fulfilled his predictions absolutely with perhaps the exception of 'low cost' and has hugely influenced our attitude to fashion and design.

However, some argue that art has lost its way. Even Charles Saatchi, one of the greatest collectors of his generation, declared art has become 'the sport of the Eurotrashy, hedgefundy Hamptonities, of trendy oligarchs and oiligarchs and of art dealers' masturbatory levels of self regard'.

Certainly, there is a widespread suspicion that art has become just another asset class with speculators manipulating prices. It is an extraordinary fact that David Geffen's $137 million purchase of a Jackson Pollock dwarfs, by a factor of 10, the world record price (paid by the Met in 2012) for a Titian. But art is still trying to answer the great philosophical questions. It's still trying to lift the spirit out of the mundane. It's the responsibility, challenge and privilege of interior designers to showcase art's power.

Martin Waller

Rose Uniacke

Rose Uniacke, London. Work is both residential and commercial from conception to completion. Current commissions include a mix of international clients. Recent projects include Estée Lauder's Jo Malone flagship office, several town houses in London and a farmhouse in the South of France. Current work includes a new build pool house, various residential houses, two commercial projects and an apartment, all in Central London. Design philosophy: fine antiques in simple, elegant, contemporary spaces. We say: masterly control of light and space makes Rose Uniacke an outstanding winner of the 2013 Award.

Jan des Bouvrie

Jan des Bouvrie. Studio Jan des Bouvrie, Naarden, The Netherlands. Predominantly high end commissions for brands such as Gelderland and Linteloo, Gamma and Princess. Jan and his team are responsible for the complete design process from start to completion. Having started at the Rietveld Design Academy, he soon developed a signature that would bring him international renown. White became Jan's favourite colour and in times of brown interiors he gave Holland light. Recent projects include a private villa in Bussum, an art exhibition at the Het Singer museum and Ricoh headquarters in Den Bosch. Design philosophy: inspire.

John Loecke & Jason Oliver Nixon. Madcap Cottage, New York, USA. A practice whose designs reflect a respect for tradition tempered with bold splashes of colour and playful patterns. Recent work includes the completion of a home in New Orleans' French Quarter, a Chinoiserie inspired guest house in Tampa and a boutique style apartment in New York City's Soho neighbourhood for the head of a major jewellery brand. Current projects include work on an English country house style cottage in New York's bucolic Catskill Mountains, a bungalow in Florida that will be packed with colour and pattern and a sophisticated NYC apartment that reflects its fashion publicist owner. Design philosophy: banish the boring and have fun. We say: extolling the joy of max.

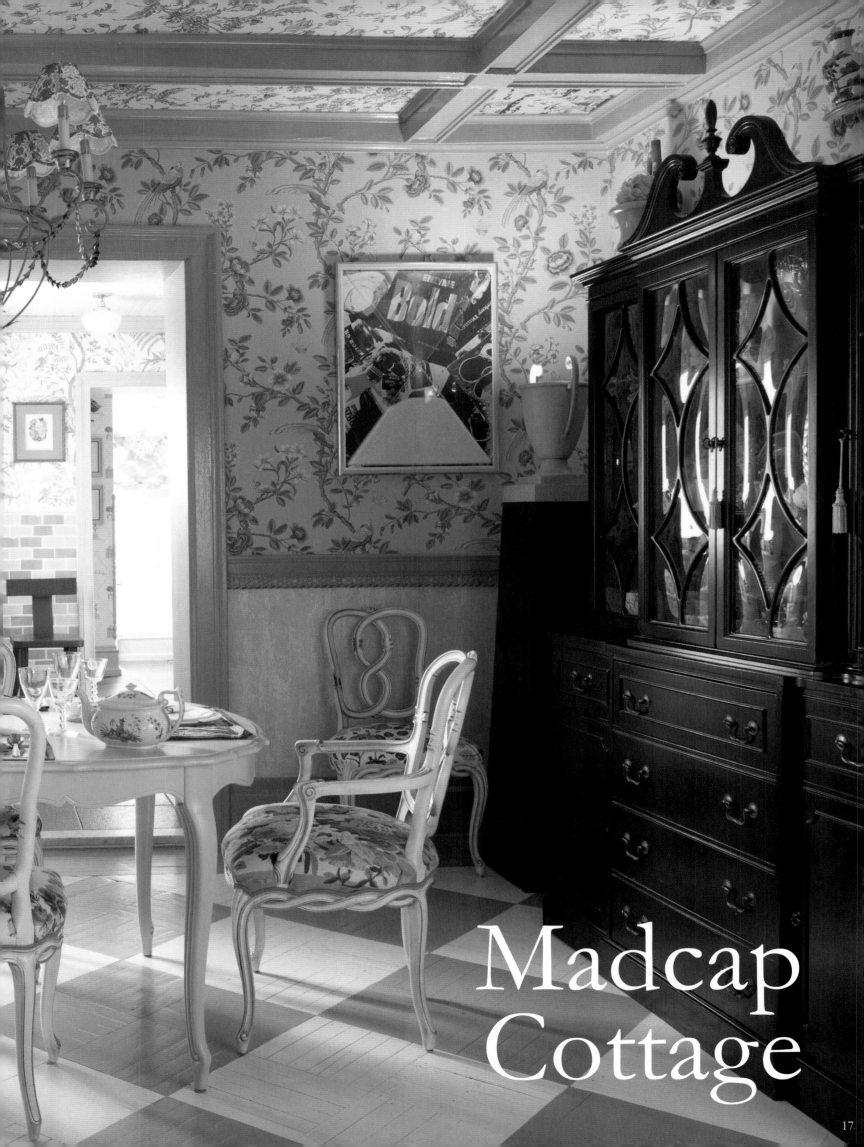

Madcap Cottage

David Scott

David Scott. David Scott Interiors, New York, USA. Recent work includes a full floor residence at the iconic Art Deco El Dorado on Central Park West in New York City, an outdoor retreat in Sagaponack, New York and an oceanfront home in Southampton, New York. Current projects include a summer residence in Sag Harbor, New York, a Lake Shore Drive apartment in Chicago, a hillside estate in Arizona; a home in Pennsylvania and the decoration of several Manhattan apartments. Design philosophy: blend the timeless elegance of the past with the functionality of the present. American paragon of sophistication.

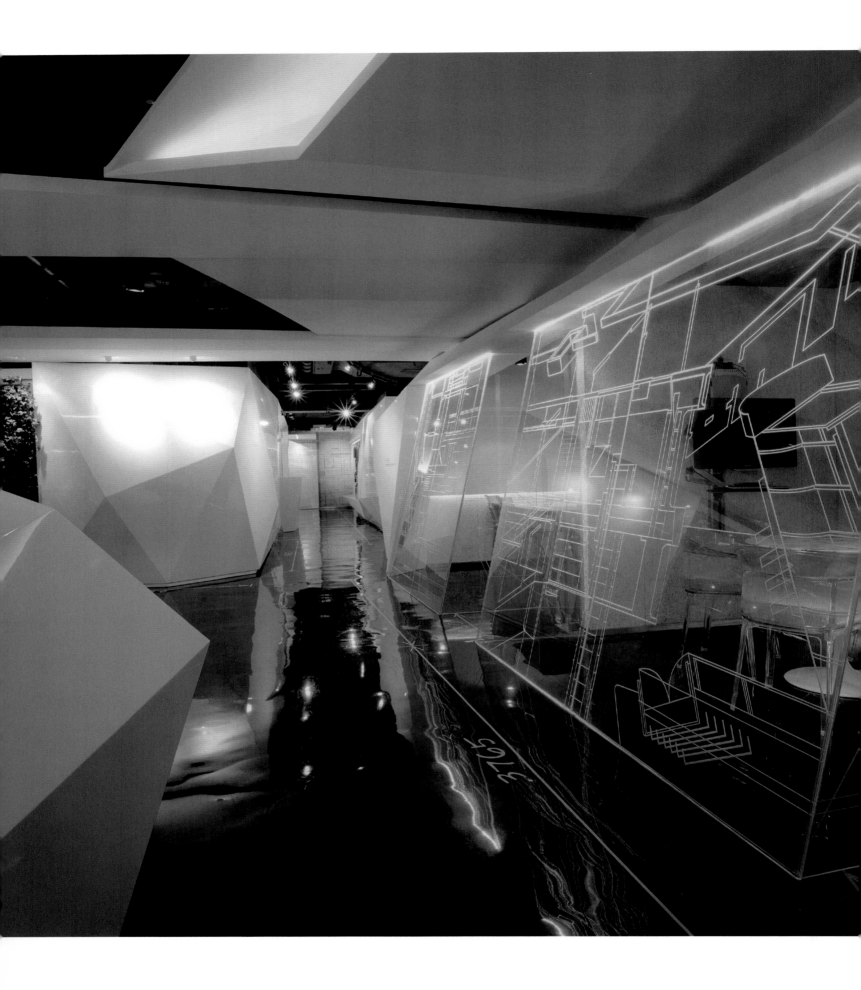

Hank M. Chao

Hank M. Chao. MoHen Design International, Shanghai, China. Specialising in interior and lighting design in Shanghai, Taiwan and Tokyo. MoHen Design create innovative schemes for residential, contract, office and hospitality design. Projects range from public buildings to interiors for private clients, with emphasis in the leisure and hospitality industry. Recent work includes an apartment in Taiwan, a boutique hotel with accents of the Chinese Han Dynasty, a maternity clinic and an office space for the digital arts. They say unexpected solutions to enhance lifestyles. We say: rising star of Chinese design.

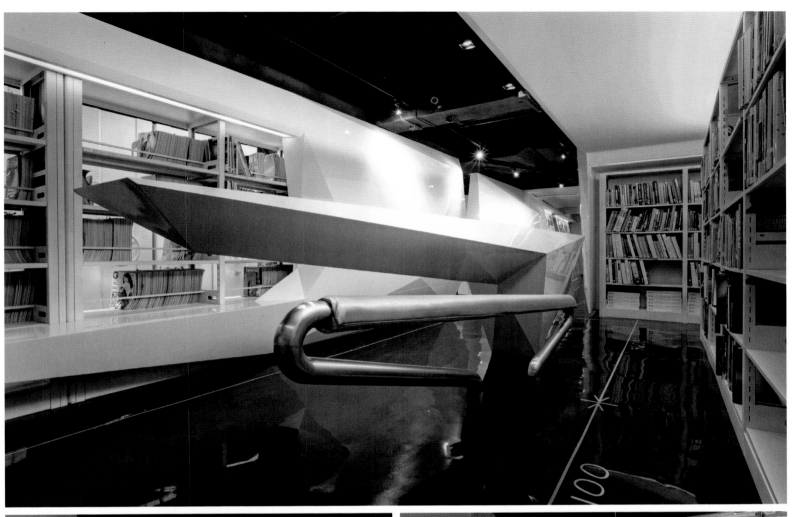

Aleksandra
Laska

Aleksandra Laska, Warsaw, Poland. Work is private and commercial, predominantly in Poland. Recent commissions include the remodeling of part of the foyer of The National Opera House in Warsaw. Current work includes a 1700 sq m showroom in a 40 story tower in Warsaw's city centre, a vintage apartment in Warsaw's old town and an installation 'a dinner for goats' in the village of Kazimierz Dolny by the Vistula River. Design philosophy: humour and individuality. We say: an Andrew Martin favourite.

Casa do Passadiço

Catarina Rosas, Cláudia Soares Pereira & Catarina Soares Pereira. Casa do Passadiço, Braga, Portugal. Predominantly bespoke residential projects. Current work includes the interior design of the lounge of a private jets company hangar, a contemporary 2500 sq m private house in Estoril facing the sea, a 2000 sq m modern villa in Vale do Lobo, Algarve, a pied à terre in an Hôtel particulier, Saint-Germain-des-Prés, Paris as well as several private houses in Portugal and abroad. Recently they were awarded in the category of 'best retail' in Europe 2012 at the International Property Awards and in Los Angeles at the International Design Awards for their interior design of a 40 metre private yacht. Design philosophy: to create luxurious yet balanced interiors.

Ana Cordeiro

Ana Cordeiro. Prego Sem Estopa, Lisbon, Portugal. Work is international, with at present several apartments in Lisbon as well as a store and a private house in Mozambique. One of Anna's most important projects is her signature design collection. In her shop, Prego Sem Estopa, she sells her wallpaper designs, lamps, furniture and other home accessories. White shades are her motto but always with splashes of colour. Design philosophy: less is more.

Blush Design

Kate Instone & Natascha Dartnall. Blush Design, London. A boutique practice that creates unique and bespoke interiors for discerning clients. Established in 2007 Blush Design have completed award winning projects for individuals and corporations in some of London's most prestigious residences. Recent work includes town houses in Belgravia and Egerton Crescent and a 3500 sq ft contemporary riverside penthouse in the Montevetro. Current projects include mansions in Upper Brook Street and Hampstead. Design philosophy: to make the client's dream a reality.

Stefano Dorata

Stefano Dorata. Studio Dorata, Rome, Italy. A boutique practice working internationally. Recent projects include a villa in Portofino, a house in London and an apartment in New York. Current work includes a hotel in Tel Aviv, a building in Sicily and a villa in London. Stefano's design philosophy is to seek classicism in contemporary values.

Kelly
Hoppen

Kelly Hoppen. Kelly Hoppen Interiors, London. A multi award winning design studio founded by Kelly Hoppen MBE. Current work includes a collaboration with Lux* Island Resorts to rejuvenate Lux* Belle Mare hotel in Mauritius, a villa in Barbados and the lobby

design and 2 show apartments of the 26 floor Topwin building featuring private residences and a hotel in Beijing. Recent projects include the contemporary interior of Pearl 75 and two show flats for Winfield Nanfung Developments in Happy Valley, Hong Kong. Working with YOO and Russian property developers Barkli Corporation, Kelly designed a show apartment, lobby and external areas of a development on Moscow's golden mile. We say: still Queen of East meets West and much more.

Jennifer Jones

Jennifer Jones. Jennifer Jones Interior Design, Johannesburg, South Africa. A small studio specialising in high end residential interiors, renovations and new builds. Recent projects in Johannesburg include a home in Craighall Park, a new build in Hurlingham and the redecoration of a house in Inanda. Current work includes a renovation in Westcliffe, the interior decoration of a home in Hurlingham and the redecoration of a residence in Illovo. Design philosophy: to create honest, simple interiors that enable comfortable, easy living with a strong awareness of the clients individuality.

Polina Belyakova, Ekaterina Grigorieva and Ekaterina Ponyatovskaya. Suite Home Interiors, Moscow, Russia. Members of the Russian Association for Interior Designers. Suite Home's portfolio consists of the interiors of apartments, houses, restaurants and offices and has been published in AD Russia and Elle Decoration. Current projects include two apartments in the centre of Moscow and a 450 sq m private mansion in the Tula region. Recent work includes a 250 sq m cottage and two further apartments in and around Moscow. Design philosophy: it's a question of taste.

Polina
Belyakova

Emma Sims-Hilditch

Emma Sims-Hilditch. Sims Hilditch, Wiltshire, UK. An award winning design practice specialising in private high end residential and commercial projects in the UK and Europe. Emma trained with Ridley Scott in film production. Her designs now combine a sense of theatre with a sympathetic use of architectural detailing, comfort and glamour. Current work includes the transformation of Grade II listed Ansty Manor, the refurbishment of the conservatory at Calcot Manor Hotel and a Grade I listed show apartment in Bath. Recent projects include the extensive refurbishment of Grade II listed Foscote Manor, an apartment in Knightsbridge and the renovation of a Queen Anne riverside townhouse. Design philosophy: preserve the architecture's authenticity, enhance the location and reflect the clients' lifestyle.

Staffan Tollgård

Staffan Tollgård. Staffan Tollgård Design Group, London. Born and raised in Stockholm, Staffan uses the Swedish expression of the 'red thread' to explain the design narrative or creative DNA that underpins every project. Recent work includes an award winning contemporary Arts & Crafts mansion in Surrey, an art collector's Belgravia apartment and an eclectic family home in Notting Hill. Currently working on a Swiss chalet, two striking architectural new builds in Berkshire and the Algarve, a couple of grand lateral conversions in Knightsbridge and refurbishments of period residences in Belgravia and Chelsea. Design philosophy: tell the client's story using the language of design.

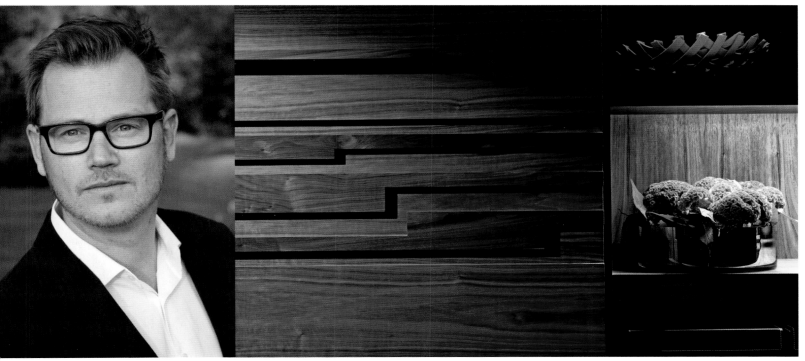

Tsimailo Lyashenko and Partners

Nikolay Lyashenko, Alexandr Tsimailo & Olga Kolesnik. Tsimailo Lyashenko and Partners, Moscow, Russia. Commercial and residential work predominantly in Moscow. Recent projects include a 4000 sq m Synagogue, a 260,000 sq m skyscraper office complex and a 217,000 sq m office centre for Danilovskaya Manufaktura all in Moscow. Current work includes 50,000 sq m of a residential project on Savvinskaya embankment, 143,250 sq m of residential buildings and a 108,400 sq m apartment centre The Park Rublevo, all in the Moscow region. Design philosophy: enjoy it (or refuse it).

Kiki
Andreou

Kiki Andreou, Marianna Vafiadis, Eleni Andreou, Faye Varvitsioti. Kiki Andreou Interiors, Athens & London. A practice which complements natural surroundings, understands the client and creates unique and elegant solutions. Recent projects include residential work in and around Athens, London and the seaside, plus the commercial office space of a 5000 sq m shipping company. Current work includes decorating short term lease apartments for international company executives.

Birgitta
Örne

Birgitta Örne. Birgitta Örne Interior Design, Stockholm, Sweden. Recent work includes several large houses on the outskirts of Stockholm. Current projects include two summerhouses in the archipelago of Stockholm, apartments in the centre and a Victorian house in London. They say 'timeless interiors in which to recharge your batteries.' We agree.

Karen Howes. Taylor Howes, London. Work is predominantly private, for London's most exclusive addresses as well as prestigious show homes, blue chip hotels and spas. Recent projects include an 11,000 sq ft church conversion behind Harrods, a contemporary finish on a William and Mary house in Richmond and a three bedroom apartment in the heart of Knightsbridge. Current work includes a house in Queensgate, a crescent house in Knightsbridge and an apartment on Grosvenor Square. Previous winners of the AM Award. Still top drawer.

Taylor Howes

Li Bo

Li Bo & Wen Jie. Cimax Design Engineering Limited, Hong Kong. Established in 2004, Cimax Design provides a diversified service led by a youthful team. Since 2008 the company has won 45 Asia-Pacific and international awards. Projects are varied including real estate, clubs, sales centres, private mansions, hotels and offices. They also offer their clients graphic design, product and architectural design. Philosophy: extract creativity from daily life.

Carmo Aranha & Rosário Tello. Sá Aranha e Vasconcelos, Portugal. An architecture and interior design studio, established in 1986. Commissions are mostly residential with some commercial plus private yachts. Recent work includes a country house outside Lisbon, a family apartment in Lisbon and a shoe shop in Zurich. Current projects include the interior design for a complex of several houses in a large rural property in Alentejo Portugal, a villa outside Lisbon and a concept store in Chiado, Lisbon. Design philosophy: make every project unique.

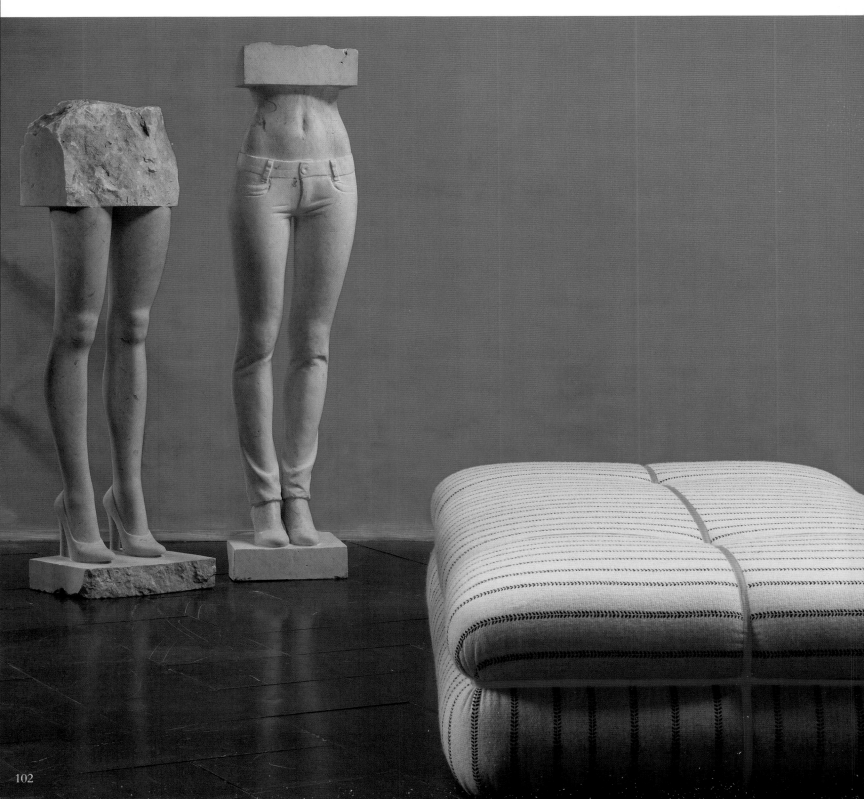

Sá Aranha
e Vasconcelos

Poppy and Charlotte O'Neil. Poco Designs, Sydney, Australia. A boutique practice established in 2009. Recent projects include numerous showcase apartments for The Stamford Group, a contemporary three level penthouse in the heart of Sydney's business district, the offices at Trivett Bespoke Showroom and an open plan waterfront property in Sydney. Current work includes a modern 3 bedroom apartment, a penthouse apartment in the heart

of Rose Bay on Sydney's harbour
and the renovation of celebrity
stylist Joh Bailey's Hair Salon.
Design philosophy: bring to life the
style, passion and imagination of
the client.

POCO
Designs

Wilkinson
Beven

John Beven & Richard Wilkinson. Wilkinson Beven, Solihull, UK. Specialising in high end private and commercial work internationally. Current projects include a new build with spa and swimming pool for a private client, a villa project in St. Tropez and contemporary concept designs for various apartments for a London developer. Recent work includes chalet 'Le Coquelicot' Courchevel 1850, a new build private villa in Barbados and the design of a tasting room at Ludlow based restaurant 'La Bécasse'. Design philosophy: understand and interpret the brief, exceed the client's requirements.

Shu
Heng
Huang

ShuHeng Huang. Sherwood Design Group, Taipei, Taiwan. An award winning practice established by ShuHeng Huang in 1998. Projects are bespoke and varied including sales centres, show flats, clubhouses, luxury villas and furniture design. Recent work is around Mainland China from Chengdu, Soo Chow to Sham Chun. Design philosophy: blend modern technology and traditional philosophy to create glamorous spaces.

Antoni
Associates

Mark Rielly & Adam Court. Antoni Associates, Cape Town, South Africa. Renowned for creating some of the most exclusive interiors in South Africa as well as international locations including London, Paris, Moscow, New York, Dubai and Geneva. Recent projects range from the refurbishment of the historic Alphen Hotel in Cape Town, a

villa on Eden Island in the Seychelles and a beach front Clifton apartment in Cape Town. Current work includes a palatial villa on Palm Jumeirah in Dubai, a penthouse apartment on Paseo de Gracia in Barcelona and a chain of hotels in Central Africa. Design philosophy: luxurious yet understated.

Finchatton

Andrew Dunn & Alex Michelin. Finchatton, London. Current work features several high end developments in London including The Connaught Penthouse adjacent to Mayfair's Connaught Hotel, a substantial private residence in Chelsea, apartment schemes in Hans Place and Cheval Place and a townhouse scheme in Yeoman's Row. International projects include a development in The Bahamas, a beach house in Mustique, a ski chalet in St Moritz and a private jet. Recent work includes the launch of The Lansbury in Knightsbridge and a boutique new build development of six apartments. Design philosophy: to create unique and exquisite homes.

Fabio Galeazzo

Fabio Galeazzo. Galeazzo Design, São Paulo, Brazil. A multidisciplinary team working in partnership with artisans to create a new vision of architecture by adding an artistic flavour to projects, going beyond form and function. Recent work includes an eco-friendly spa, a design hotel in São Paulo and a conceptual space for an internet company. Current projects include an important cookery school and French restaurants, a home studio for a sculptor and a new design concept for a farm experience hotel. Galeazzo's design philosophy: understand human behaviour.

Chou Yi

Chou Yi. Joy-Chou Yi Interior Design Studio, Taichung City, Taiwan. An award winning practice established in 1989. Major projects include tea houses and restaurants including Chuan-Shua Tang and Han-Lin tea houses, Hakka, Kazusawa and Er-Bu Yuan restaurants plus Tai-Chu noodle restaurant. Current projects include the Puhui reception centre, The Pot restaurant and The Peach Blossom restaurant. Design philosophy: imaginative with space, never compromise on detail.

Scott Sanders

Scott Sanders, New York, USA. Founded in 2000, Scott Sanders LLC is a full service New York City and Hamptons based interior design firm focused on creating sophisticated yet approachable interiors that epitomise the Sanders' signature fresh American style. His portfolio includes homes in New York City, the Hamptons, New Jersey, Colorado, Arizona, Florida and the Caribbean. Current projects include a penthouse apartment in Manhattan, a historic home in the foothills of the Catalina Mountains in Tucson and the corporate offices, retail shop, café and tour spaces for a maple syrup company in Duchess County, NY. Design philosophy: listen to the client's needs, tailor the environment to reflect them. We say: wise and witty.

Nikki Hunt

Nikki Hunt. Design Intervention, Singapore. An international team of 24, made up of 12 different nationalities. Work is tailor made for a diverse clientele spanning five continents. Projects are varied: London apartments, Bali villas, holiday retreats in the French countryside and Swiss Alps, beach homes in Australia and ski lodges in Japan. Current work includes a penthouse apartment in Singapore, a family home in Kuala Lumpur and a hotel in Japan.

Les Interieurs

Pamela Makin. Les Interieurs, Sydney, Australia. Current projects include a seafront house in Palm Beach and a city apartment overlooking Sydney Harbour. Recent work includes the complete restoration of a penthouse in Sydney, the interiors of an estate in Balmoral and a three storey contemporary residence in Bayview. Pamela's design philosophy is to enhance architectural form and space with an eclectic mix of contemporary furniture, interesting artefacts and found objects. We say: classy and cool.

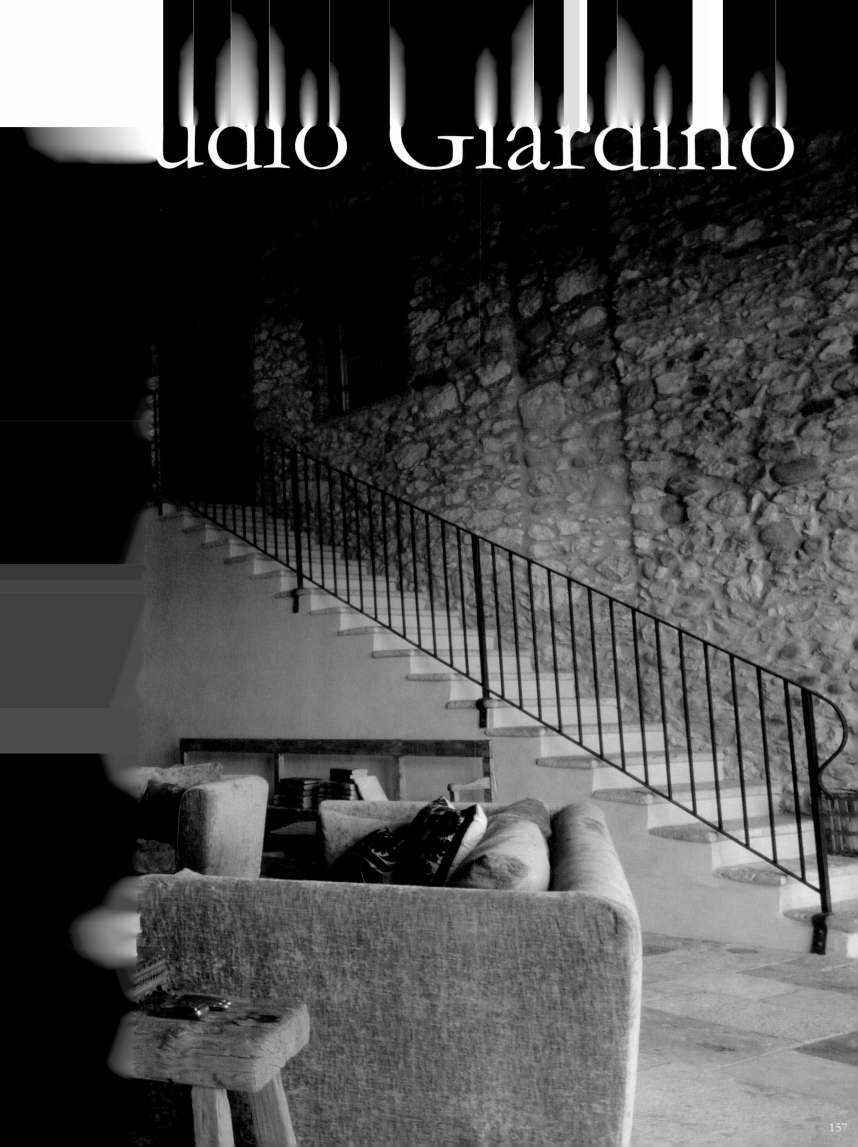

Studio Giardino

Enrica Fiorentini Delpani. Studio Giardino, Brescia, Italy. Specialising in interior design and architecture throughout Italy as well as internationally. Recent projects include an old country villa, apartments in Milan and a house in the mountains. Current work includes a house in Ramatuelle, Cote d'Azur and a hotel and spa on Lake Garda. Enrica's design philosophy is to renovate with respect. We say: timeless.

March
& White

Elliot March & James White. March & White, London. Founded by Elliot March and James White, commissions include the design of private residences, hotels, restaurants, members' clubs and super yachts. Current projects range from a penthouse duplex apartment in the heart of Chelsea, a super yacht and a large beach house in the Middle East. Recent work includes Lima, a Peruvian restaurant in Fitzrovia, an apart'hotel for Go Native, with 63 apartments adjacent to London's Hyde Park and a modern reinvention of a London coach house. Design philosophy: tailor made to reflect the client's objectives.

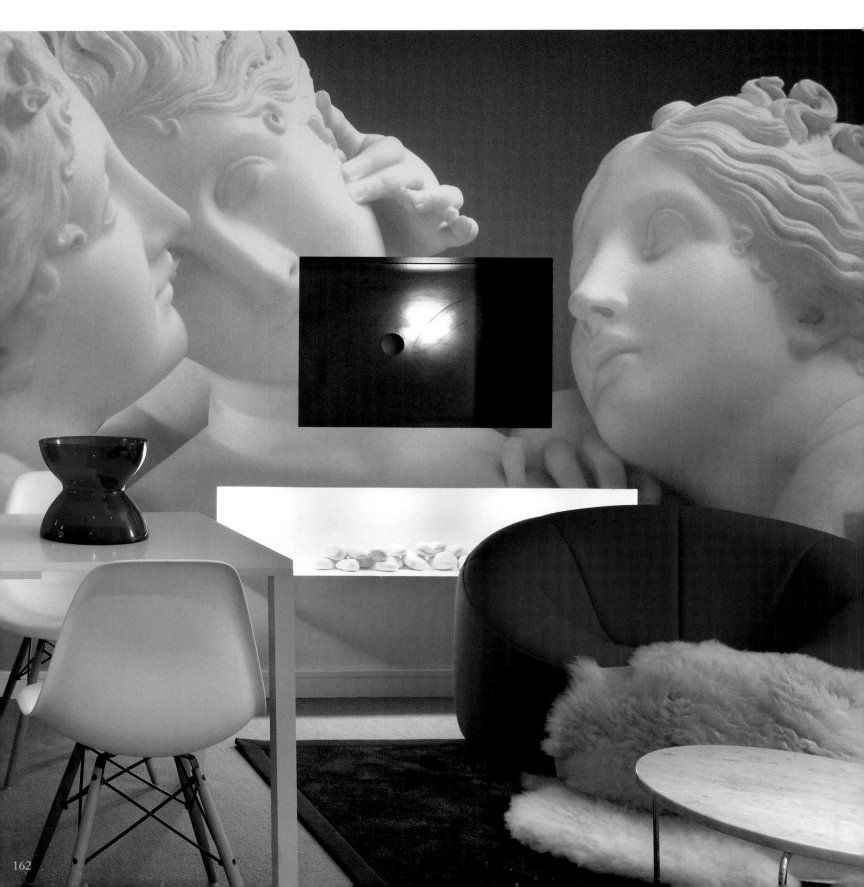

Roy Teo

Roy Teo. Kri:eit Associates, Singapore. Founded by renowned designer Roy Teo, Kri:eit is an award winning practice with clients including Hollywood star Jet Li. Recent projects include a pied à terre at Marina Bay Residences, as well as Singapore's Chatsworth House. Current work includes spearheading the design of a residence in the Nassim Hill quarter and the enigmatic, emerald green studded Billionaire headquarters at Stanley Street. Design philosophy: reinvent in the name of bespoke design.

Dimore

Lucia Valzelli. Dimore, Brescia, Italy. Work is exclusive, predominantly residential and tailor made, including hotels and spas in Northern Italy but also internationally. Recent projects include a villa on Lake Geneva, the renovation of a modern country house and a large private villa in the Carribean. Current work includes the complete design for a high end residential eco project with twenty flats in Lombardy, a penthouse and a modern flat in the heart of Milan. Design philosophy: to create clean, simple design with a sense of quiet luxury.

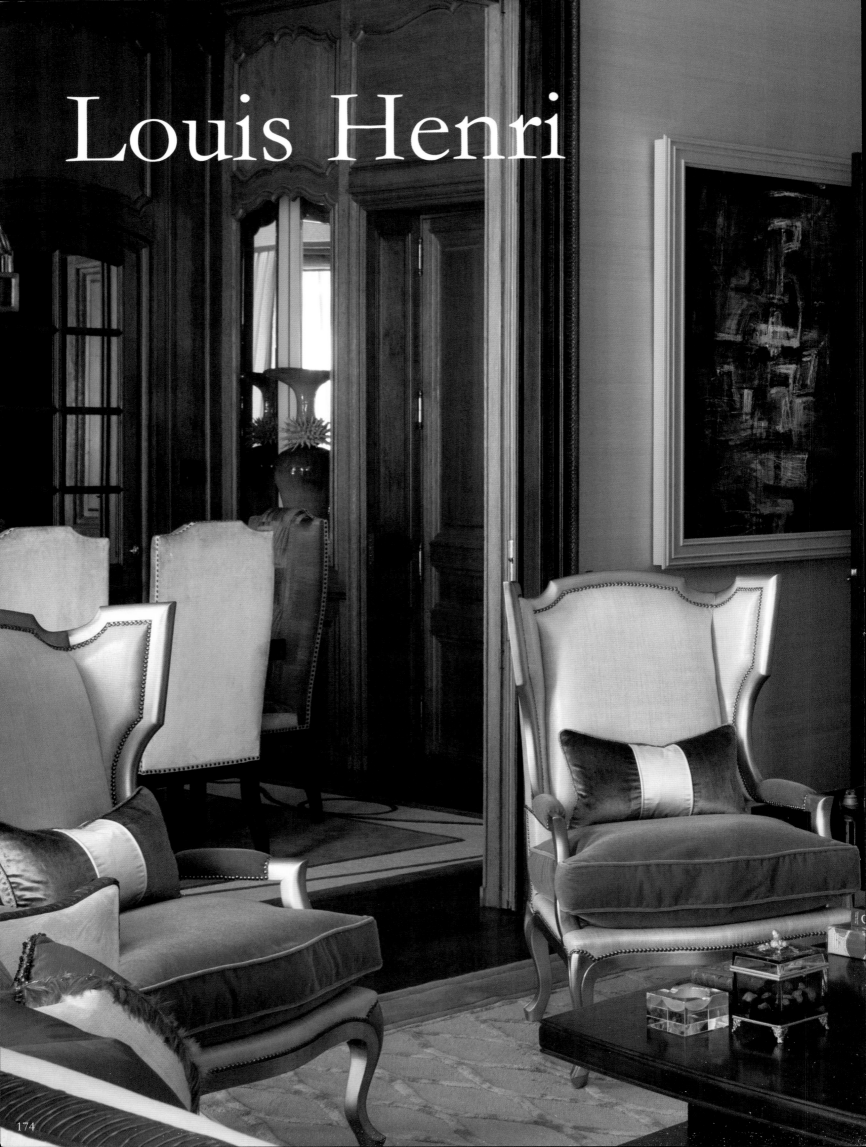

Louis Henri

Louis Bührmann. Louis Henri Ltd, London. South African born director, Louis Henri Bührmann runs a boutique firm specialising in luxurious, residential interiors. He also designs a collection of limited edition furniture, lighting, accessories and artwork. Pieces are bespoke, over scaled, whimsical and inspired by nature. Recent projects include a luxurious five bedroom lateral apartment in Paris' Avenue Montaigne, a family home in Mayfair which serves as a backdrop to an extensive modern art collection and a holiday home in Antibes, South of France. Current projects include the complete remodeling of a generously proportioned period property in Knightsbridge. Design philosophy: affinity for luxury.

Jordivayreda

Projectteam

Jordi Vayreda. Jordivayreda Projectteam, Catalonia, Spain. Residential and commercial work plus product and furniture design. Recent commissions include Michelin starred restaurants Ca l'Enric in Catalonia and Asador Etxebarri in Euskadi as well as retail environments such as clothes shops, beauticians and a spa and various residential spaces throughout Catalonia. Current projects include the development of new design concepts for villas in the Mediterranean and several corporate projects for major companies in differing sectors. Mantra: know how to listen.

Jenny Weiss & Helen Bygraves. Hill House Interiors, Surrey, UK. Bespoke commissions specialising in the complete design of luxury show houses and private residences in the UK and overseas. Current work includes large country estates in Kazakhstan and the Isle of Man as well as a penthouse apartment in Chelsea. Recent projects include a regency house in Belgravia, a modern mansion in St George's Hill and the refurbishment of a substantial town house overlooking Hyde Park. Design philosophy: tailor made aspirational design without compromise.

Danny Cheng

Danny Cheng. Danny Cheng Interiors Limited, Hong Kong. Danny Cheng is a graduate of Toronto's International Academy of Merchandising and Design. He began his design career in Hong Kong in 1996 and set up his business Danny Cheng Interiors in 2002. Throughout his 16 years of design profession he advocates for minimalism, linear aesthetics and spatial generosity. Commissions are predominantly residential including show flat designs and commercial designs for the Bang & Olufsen showrooms and apartments for developers including Base Keen Investment Ltd, Henderson Land Development Ltd and HKR International Ltd. Design philosophy: simple but good.

Sera of London

Sera Hersham. Sera of London, London. Recent projects include the set design for BBC World News, the launch of her book Seductive Interiors and the interior design for a fleet of private jets. Current work includes a beach house in Ibiza, an apartment in Little Venice and the interiors of a set of glamorous tents for this summer's music festivals. They say 'homes with soul.' We say: the mistress of bohemian rock 'n' roll.

Jorge
Cañete

Jorge Cañete. Interior Design Philosophy, Switzerland. Having opened his studio in 2006, the company specialises in both residential and commercial design. Recent projects include an 18th century castle near Lausanne, a chalet in the Swiss Alps and two art exhibitions: Isa Barbier and Silvana Solivella. Current work includes villas overlooking Lake Geneva, a restaurant and lounge in Lausanne and a new art exhibition with French artist Marie Ducaté. Design philosophy: preserve historical architecture by creating harmony between interior and exterior spaces. We say: always original often magical.

Holger Kaus

Holger Kaus. Holger Kaus Design, Tegernsee, Germany. A boutique practice located in the Bavarian countryside, where client presentations are hosted in a quiet, traditional setting. Work is predominantly residential. Current projects include a house in the Swiss Alps, a castle in Austria and an eccentric early 20th century villa in Berlin. Recent work includes various apartments throughout Europe. Design philosophy: nature is inspiration.

Geometry

Irina Glik. Geometry, Moscow, Russia. Specialising in high end private and commercial work in Russia as well as internationally. Recent projects include Novikov Restaurant and Bar, London, La Bottega Siciliana di Nino Graziano, Moscow and Strana kotoroy net, Moscow. Current work includes a private residence in Monaco, an office centre in Moscow and Brompton Asian Brasserie London. Design philosophy: embed timeless elements with modern technology.

Gauthier-Stacy

Jim Gauthier & Susan Stacy. Gauthier-Stacy, Boston, USA. A boutique practice established in 1996, Gauthier-Stacy specialise in high end residential with some commercial interior projects throughout the United States. Recent work includes CRU Oyster Bar, a 114 seat bar and restaurant situated at the harbour's edge in Nantucket, Massachusetts, a new 6,600 sq ft home on John's Island in Florida and a penthouse overlooking Central Park in New York. Current projects include a 4,500 sq ft cottage in Key Largo, Florida, Finagle A Bagel World Headquarters restaurant/outlet store in Massachusetts, a 9,500 sq ft Antebellum estate on Cape Cod and a 3,500 sq ft contemporary apartment in Montreal. Design philosophy: exceed expectations.

Chang Ching-Ping

Chang Ching-Ping. Tien Fun Interior Planning, Taichung, Taiwan. Established in 1988 at Tienmu, Taiwan and now with roots in Taichung, Tien Fun specialise in high end residential and show flats, landscape design, public area space planning, furniture and office design throughout Asia. The team consists of more than 20 experienced designers working in varied styles including Asian, classic, modern and retro. Recent projects include Alexandre furniture showroom in Shanghai, the lobby area of Glory Tower in Taichung and a residence also in Taichung. Design philosophy: high quality design and high quality craftsmanship. We say: spectacular.

One Plus Partnership

Ajax Law & Virginia Lung. One Plus Partnership Ltd, Hong Kong. Established in 2004, the name One Plus is derived from number 'one' which refers to the partners' unity and 'plus' which refers to everyone who contributes to the success of each project. Commissions are both commercial and private throughout Asia. Recent projects include their own office, Tianjin Insun Lotte Cinema and Chongqing Flower and City Sales Office. Current work includes a clubhouse, sales office, lobbies, show flats and a shopping space for a residential development in Shenzhen, a movie theatre in a prime shopping mall in Hong Kong and a sales office in Central, Hong Kong. Design philosophy: to create cutting edge design. We say: brilliant winners of the 2012 AM Design Award.

Apartment 9

Mayank Gupta. Apartment 9, New Delhi, India. The design arm of the company was established in 2006. With furniture design and production in house, the entire team plan, develop, process and deliver their solutions. Current projects range in size from 5000 sq ft to 25,000 sq ft with homes in Northern India, in Lutyens Delhi and several in South Delhi and the outskirts, the family home of a famous business group in Kanpur, a café in South Delhi and a designer retail store. Design philosophy: 'aplomb without apology.'

Hecker Guthrie

Paul Hecker & Hamish Guthrie. Hecker Guthrie, Melbourne, Australia. A multi disciplinary design practice. Work is both local and overseas with current projects focusing on the hospitality, residential, retail and commercial sectors. Paul Hecker and Hamish Guthrie are highly respected representatives of the Australian design community and their work is regularly published in design and lifestyle journals, books and blogs. Recent work includes Foxes Den restaurant, Evie apartments and The Beach Club in Perth. Current projects include a Yarradale Road residence, the executive offices for Built and Elwood retail stores. Design philosophy: authenticity, consideration, enthusiasm.

Krista Hartmann

Krista Hartmann. Krista Hartmann Interior AS, Oslo, Norway. A boutique practice with an exclusive sewing studio. Current work includes a luxury bed linen shop and an office in Oslo, a winter house in the Norwegian mountains and a private residence with spa and fitness area next to the Oslo fjord. Recent projects include several winter houses in different mountain resorts, a luxury hunting lodge in the depths of the forest and the renovation of an old summerhouse in the South of Norway. Design philosophy: to perfectly combine aesthetic with comfort.

Decoration Empire

Thong Lei & Anne Noordam. Decoration Empire, Gouda, The Netherlands. Offering a full design service with a strong client rapport. Recent projects include a 19th century castle, an apartment in Faubourg St Honoré to house the owner's art collection and a penthouse in The Hague. Current work includes the complete refurbishment of an 18th century ruin in Riga into a 5 star hotel, the design and rebuild of an early 20th century house in Amsterdam and a late 19th century villa in Hamburg. Design philosophy: unique homes with soul.

Intarya

Daniel Kostiuc & team. Intarya, London. Recent projects include a Notting Hill penthouse as well as show apartments and private residences at The Lancasters, overlooking Hyde Park. Their current portfolio includes architectural and interior design projects in Kensington, Knightsbridge, Belgravia and Notting Hill. Intarya's philosophy is to sympathetically and imperceptibly blend the new with the original while creating memorable interiors. We say: the practice that helped define the London look.

Glamorous

Yasumichi Morita. Glamorous Design, Tokyo, Japan. Established in 2000 by Yasumichi Morita, work is expanding to cities globally including New York, London and Shanghai. As well as interior design, work extends to graphic and product design. Recent projects include the remodeling of the main building of Isetan Shinjuku department store, Tokyo, the office entrance, lobby lounge and sales centre of Fantasia Future Plaza, Chengdu, China and lounge bar '1967' in Tokyo. Current projects include the redevelopment of Arashiyama concourse, Kyoto's favourite station, Japanese restaurant Morimoto, Miami and Social Club wine bar in Doha, Qatar.

Roy Azar

Roy Azar. Roy Azar Architects, Mexico City. Work is for an elite clientele. Recent projects include the company's own Tribeca loft inspired design studio including meeting space, living area and private terrace, each area surrounded by the owner's collection of art, L'Ôtel in San Miguel de Allende, Mexico, a boutique hotel conceived as a sanctuary and The St Regis Punta Mita Resort on the Pacific Coast. Current projects include the interior architecture for Mítikah, a multi-purpose development for entertainment, culture and lifestyle, Frondoso, a 5000 sq ft apartment outside Mexico City and the complete renovation of an 8000 sq ft Sierra Vertientes Residence. Design Philosophy: balance and harmony, natural light, generous spaces and a neutral palette.

Candy & Candy

Nick Candy. Candy & Candy, London. Founded in 1999, Candy & Candy is dedicated to designing the most luxurious real estate. Current projects include The Penthouse at One Hyde Park, London with its own spa, home cinema, games room and gymnasium, The Penthouse at The Plaza Hotel, New York and The Penthouse, Arlington Street above The Wolseley restaurant, featuring two large roof terraces with 360 degree views over London. Design philosophy: the pursuit of perfection.

Bin Wu

Bin Wu. Hong Kong W. Architectural Design, Shanghai, China. Since 1993 Bin has specialised in hotels, clubs and private residences. Recent work includes the Aerial Club of MIXC Mall in Hangzhou and The Imperial Garden Villa in Shanghai. Current projects include Shanghai Portman JYL and Ningbo Fortune Center. Firmly established as part of the new wave of China's designers.

Hare+Klein

Meryl Hare. Hare + Klein, Sydney, Australia. Recipients of 7 major Australian Design Awards, Hare + Klein specialise in residential and hospitality. Recent projects include the refurbishment of villas on Hamilton Island, the completion of a large heritage residence in Sydney and an international finance company headquarters in Sydney. Current projects include a 5 star luxury boutique hotel on Hamilton Island, a restaurant complex for Hilton Hotels in Fiji and new private residences in Sydney, Darwin and Adelaide. Design philosophy: comfortable, appropriate and individual.

Ivan Cheng

Ivan Cheng. Ivan C Design, Hong Kong. Specialising in luxury design for 5 star hotels, villas and show flats that combine classical elements with modern concepts. Recent projects include Wen Xi Louis Garden Clubhouse and show flats, The City Star Clubhouse and show flats and Triumphal Arch Sale office, all in Hangzhou. Current work includes Xixi Pearl Clubhouse and Villas Hangzhou, Jiangmen Villa, Guangzhou Pearl River and Tianyi Green Ocean private Club house, Tianjin. Design philosophy: to create timeless interiors with bold statements. We say: at the forefront of China's new wave.

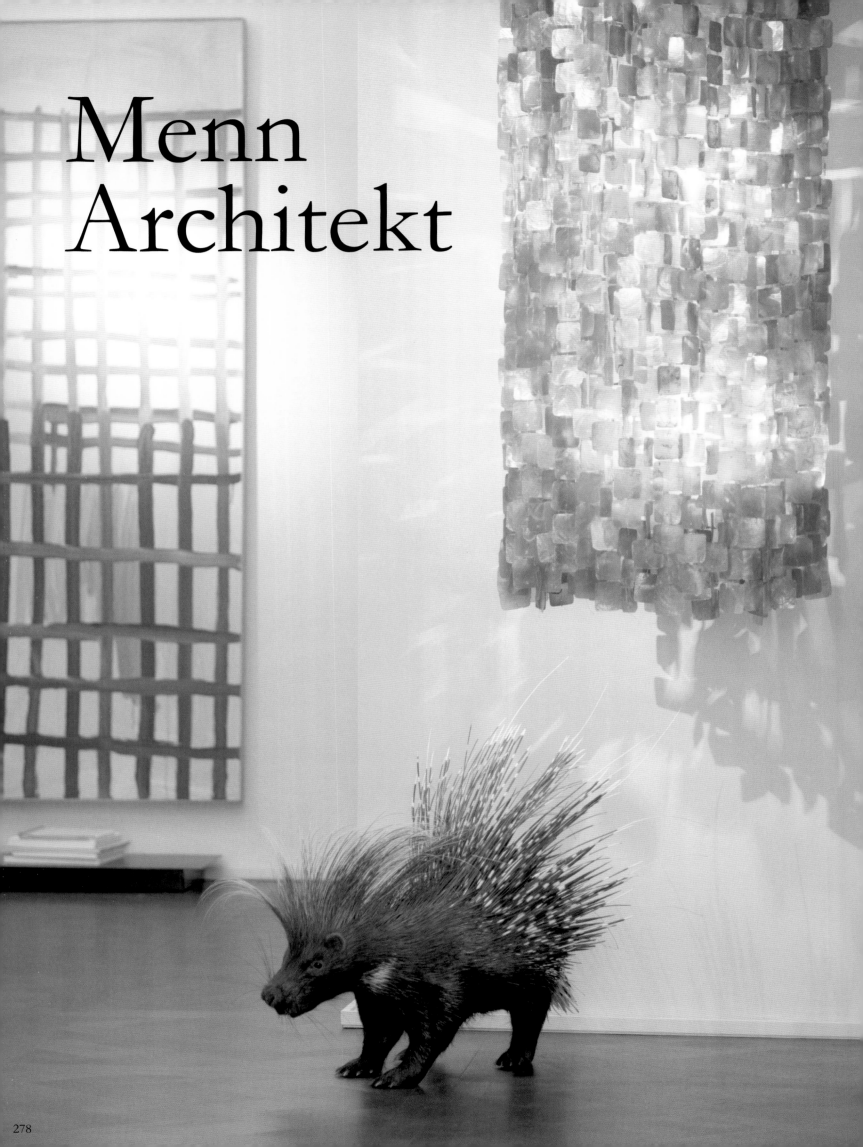

Menn
Architekt

Stephan Menn & Marc Neise. Menn Architekt & Fausel Biskamp, Düsseldorf, Germany. Founded in 1887, as well as interior and architectural design the practice also has its own range of high end wall coverings. Recent projects include Adlon, Berlin, Breuninger, a training course village for SMS Demag and the private apartment for the owner of Pears Group, Kuwait. Current work includes 'The Breidenbacher Hof' a high end hotel in Düsseldorf, a holiday house for a German businessman, plus residential projects for two Russian families.

Federica Palacios

Federica Palacios. Federica Palacios Design, Geneva, Switzerland. A small practice working on predominantly private work internationally. Recent projects include exclusive apartments in Alpina Gstaad, a Geneva duplex and a summer house in the South of France. Current work includes an apartment in Miami, a loft in Monaco and the restoration of a barn in Gstaad. They say: less is more. We say: perennial chic.

Alan Chan

Alan Chan. Alan Chan Design Company, Hong Kong. Offering a total branding solution from visual identity, interior design and architecture to art consultancy. Recent work includes the 3 Michelin starred French restaurant Robuchon au Dome in Macau, a zen vegetarian flagship restaurant Suchengzhai in Guangzhou and a clubhouse refurbished from a 600 year old Imperial Granary in Beijing. Design philosophy: to fuse Oriental and Western culture through a modern perspective. We say: compelling creators of drama.

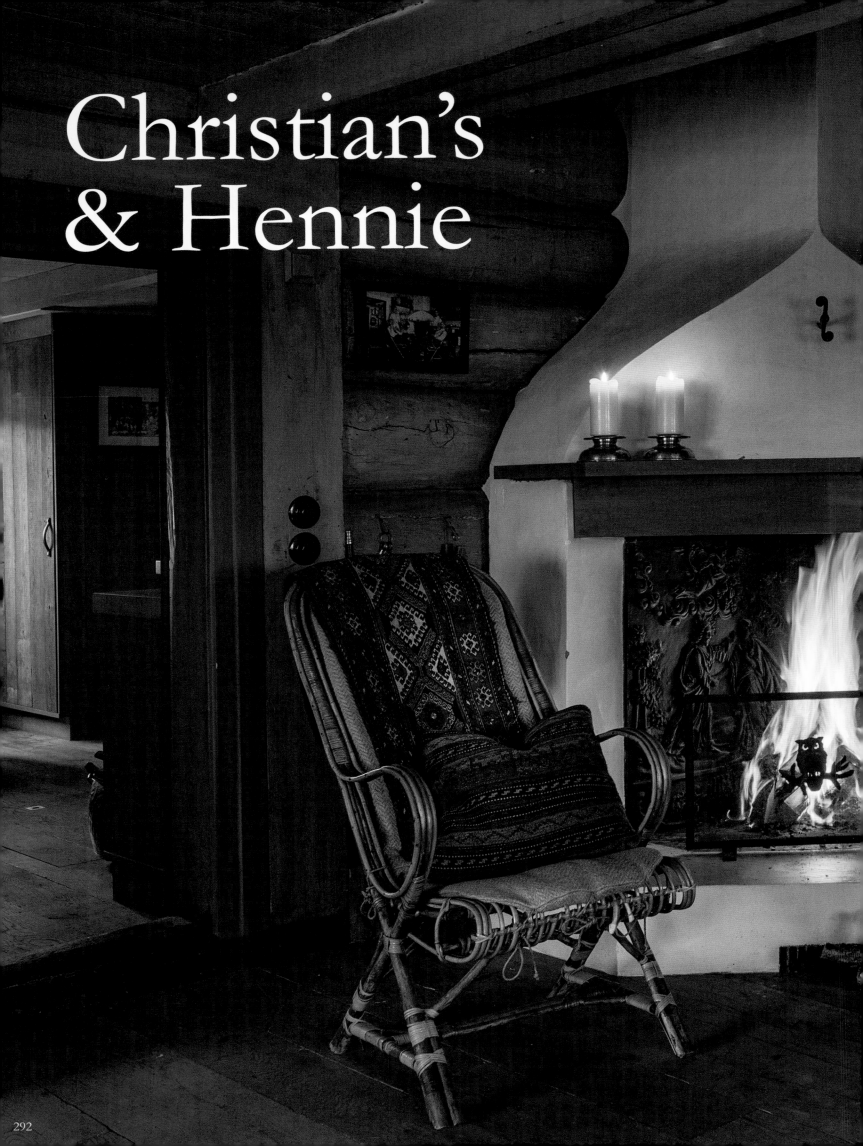

Christian's
& Hennie

Helene Hennie. Christian's & Hennie, Oslo, Norway. Helene and her well established team projects reflect extensive experience in creating high end livable spaces for international clients. Projects are both commercial and private ranging from winter lodges, summer cabins and city apartments to offices and restaurants. Current work includes a private modern residence in Singapore, a classic summerhouse along the coast of Norway and a sleek Pied à Terre in Marbella. Helene's philosophy is to create elegant, comfortable and individual interiors with a style that varies from modern to classical. We say: Helene Hennie is Norway's pre eminent designer.

CHRISTIAN'S & HENNIE

Erginoglu
& Çalislar

Hasan Çalislar and Kerem Erginoglu. Erginoglu & Çalislar Architects, Istanbul, Turkey. An independent firm of architects founded in 1993, specialising in urban planning, architecture and interior design. Recent projects include the conversion of 2000 sq m Yemeksepeti offices, the 5000 sq m structural transformation of workspace for TBWA creative advertising agency in Istanbul and the offices of Sahibinden online shopping platform. Current work includes a family house; a renovation project on the Bosphorus, a BP office project in Istanbul and Anadolu insurance company offices in Istanbul. Design philosophy: innovative solutions within individual context.

Nihal Zaki

Nihal Zaki. Nihal Zaki Interiors, Cairo, Egypt. Founded in 2002, specialising in residential and commercial interior design plus events styling and art direction. Recent projects include 'Ylounge' a Lebanese restaurant and club lounge located on a 500 sq m rooftop of a boat by the banks of the river Nile, the restaurant 'el Shagara' and the art direction for a series of Nostalgia themed events commissioned by Tamari, Cairo's number one nightspot. Current work includes a 2000 sq m private residence in the suburbs of Cairo, the modern design of Dubai based Capital Investment offices in Cairo. The latest project, a 'Baroque gone bad' themed charity ball at one of Cairo's renowned boutique hotels.

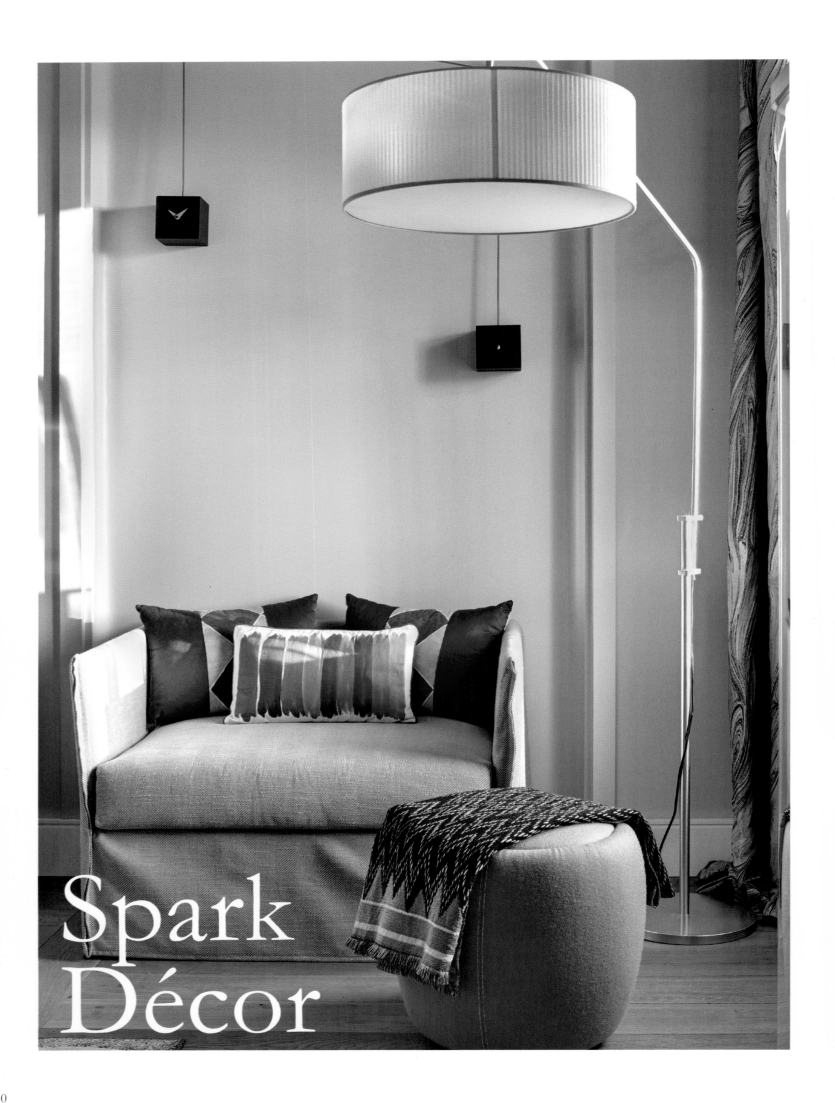

Spark
Décor

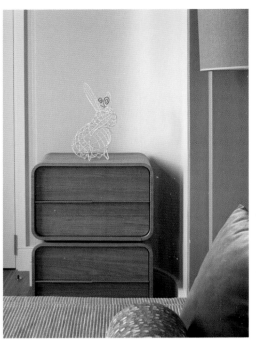

Madina Vykhodtseva. Spark Décor, Moscow, Russia. Established in 2004, Spark Décor focuses on the design of private and commercial work that reflects the client. Recent projects are all in Moscow and include three country houses. Current work includes two apartments and a small hotel. Design philosophy: simple, elegant, comfortable.

Angelos Angelopoulos

Angelos Angelopoulos, Athens, Greece. Commissions are private and commercial including residences, apartments, restaurants, clubs, hotels, showrooms and work spaces predominantly in Athens as well as Cyprus, Istanbul and the USA. In the 90's Angelos designed the first boutique hotel of its kind in Athens, since then he has designed the interiors of more than 40 hotels. Recent work includes a new seafront resort in Cyprus, a Japanese and beach restaurant, the restoration and renovation of an old mansion in Attica and a new mountain resort in Greece. Current projects include a penthouse with roof garden in Athens, exclusive VIP villas in a seaside resort in Cyprus and a private residence by the ocean in Florida. Design philosophy: the inspiration is the client. We say: a groundbreaking talent.

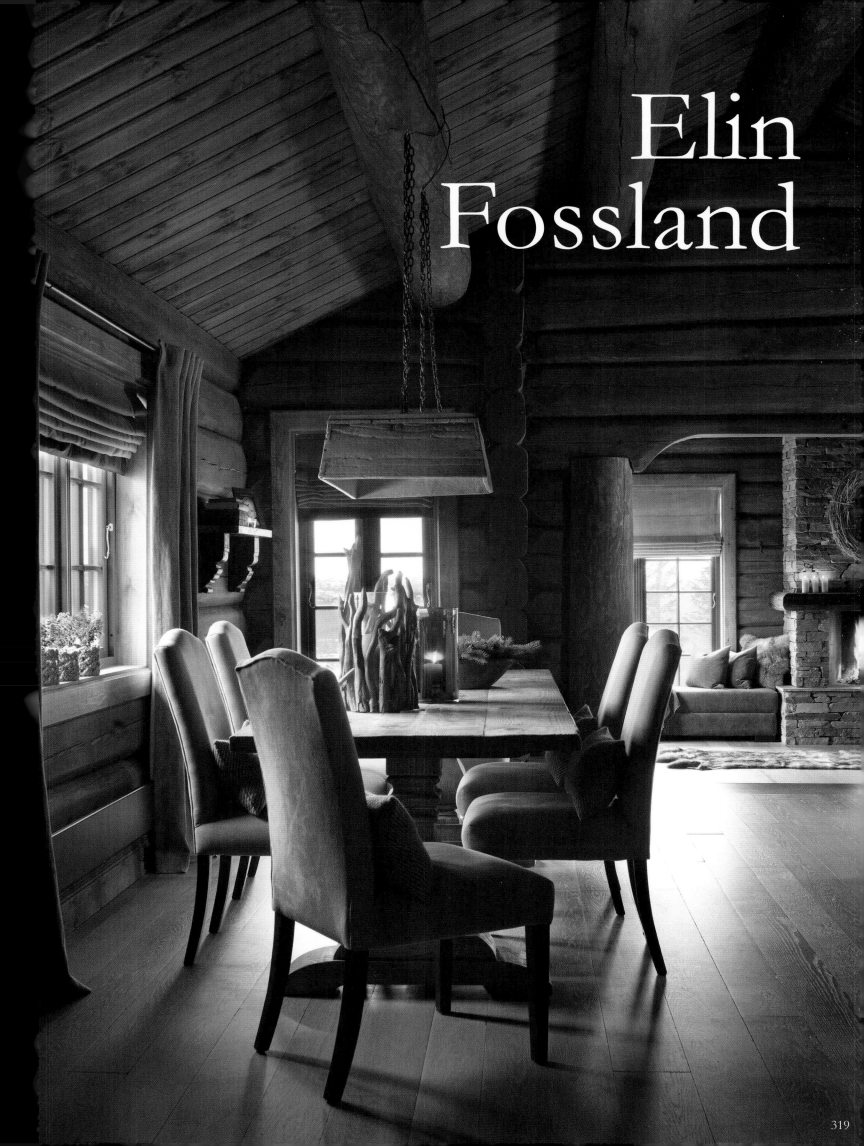

Elin
Fossland

Elin Fossland. Arkitektfossland AS, Drammen, Norway. A small company specialising in private residences and chalets as well as public and office interiors in Norway and abroad. Recent projects include a waterfront office building in Oslo, a private residence in Drammen and a holiday home in the Norwegian mountains. Current work includes a mountain restaurant in Geilo, Norway and a Funkis house in Oslo. Elin's philosophy is to create interiors with personality by combining new design and antiques with a soft muted palette.

Ken Freivokh

Ken Freivokh. Ken Freivokh Design, Hampshire, UK. Specialising in the design of motor and sailing yachts and private jets. Current work includes the largest sailing yacht in the world, a 141m four mast schooner, a 145m turbine powered motor yacht and the interiors for a range of semi production powerboats. The KFD team has been responsible for most Sunseeker interiors over the past 20 years. Recent notable projects include the 88m DynaRIG yacht 'Maltese Falcon', the largest privately owned sailing yacht in the world, 'Quinta Essentia' a 55m Heesen yacht launched in 2011 and crowned 'Queen of Monaco' plus a Global Express jet for the chairman of Bombardier. Design philosophy: lateral thinking and out-of-the-box solutions.

Kathleen Hay

Kathleen Hay. Kathleen Hay Designs, Nantucket, USA. New construction is a specialty, with an emphasis on high end residential and commercial design. Recent projects include a private ski lodge set in 69 acres located on the highest point in Woodstock, Vermont, a state of the art music school complete with advanced sound considerations, live room, mixing studio and teaching studios as well as performance spaces, a boutique hotel on Nantucket Island and a jet setters paradise on the Northeast coast of the US. Design philosophy: fresh, sophisticated, contemporary.

Atsuhiko Sugiyama

Atsuhiko Sugiyama. The Wholedesign Inc, Tokyo, Japan. Specialising in high end hospitality, commercial, residential and furniture design in Japan. Recent projects include Tomori rooftop bar in Tokyo, the dining and entertaining space at Bleu Leman in Nagoya City and Heigoro patisserie in Nagano. Current work includes Kawabun restaurant Nagoya, the renovation of Japonais restaurant and wedding hall in Nigata and Luigans restaurant and reception area in Fukuoka. Philosophy: design the best.

Martyn Lawrence Bullard

Martyn Lawrence Bullard. Martyn Lawrence Bullard Design, California, USA. Known as the designer to the stars Martyn's clients include Sir Elton John and David Furnish, Cher, Eva Mendes, Nicki Minaj, Tommy Hilfiger, Sharon & Ozzy Osbourne, Kid Rock, Edward Norton, Christina Aguilera, he also works on hotels and shops worldwide including the Kona Village resort in Kona, Hawaii, the Californian Hotel in Santa Barbara and Jimmy Choo stores. Martyn is also the star of Bravo televisions 'million dollar decorator' in the US and Channel 4's 'Hollywood Me' in the UK. Recent work includes a new home for Sir Elton John in Los Angeles, a 12th century castle in Umbria, Italy and a Balinese style villa on the beach in Malibu. He is currently working on the famous Chateau Gütsch in Lucerne, an ultra modern beach house in Miami for Tommy Hilfiger and a historically important Tuscan style villa in the Hollywood hills for star Ellen Pompeo. Design philosophy: constant travel feeds diversity and creativity.

343

Tsung-Jen Lin

Tsung-Jen Lin, Crox International, Shanghai, China. Specialising in architecture and urban planning with projects ranging from window displays, scenery and interiors to large scale exhibitions and urban landscape. Recent projects include La Lé Wine Bar in Shanghai and One Taste Holistic Health Club situated in the mountains between Hangzhou City's Chenghuang Temple and the West Lake, China. Current work includes the Avant Garde design of Wuhan Echo Club. Design philosophy: redefine traditional space.

Hugh
Leslie

Hugh Leslie. Hugh Leslie Design, London. Hugh studied design and interior architecture in New Zealand before coming to England. His practice is now in its 10th year and projects range from London houses, apartments, country houses and homes abroad. Hugh's work is a constant collaboration with his client's desires and aspirations. Current projects include a house in Manhattan, a Hampshire estate and various projects in London. Recently completed works include a chalet in Switzerland, a country house in Oxfordshire and a terraced house in Chelsea. Design philosophy: create the perfect home for the client.

Linda Steen

Linda Steen. AS Scenario, Oslo, Norway. Founded in 1984 by Linda Steen, Scenario interiørarkitekter MNIL is today one of Norway's largest practices. With a staff of 26 interior architects, projects include hotels, homes, shops, offices and furniture design. Recent projects include the eighteen story Rica Hotel Narvik, the rebranding for Diplom- is, a Norwegian ice cream company and the 40,000 sq m new offices for Aker solutions engineering company. Current work also includes several private residences, offices and the new National library Deichman. Design philosophy: design the best for tomorrow's workflow.

Steve
Leung

Steve Leung. Steve Leung Designers, Hong Kong. Consisting of a team of 350 designers who specialise in residential, commercial and hospitality design projects. Recent work includes Yoo Residence, 39 Conduit Road and Mango Tree in

Hong Kong. Current work includes a hotel in London, a residential development project in Singapore and a resort hotel in Sanya, China. Design philosophy: enjoy life and enjoy design. We say: one of Hong Kong's most respected designers.

Rachel
Laxer

Rachel Laxer. Rachel Laxer Interiors, London. Founded in 2007 and currently with offices in New York and London. With an international lifestyle and viewpoint that spans Europe, Asia and the United States, Rachel creates interiors marked by a signature style that is luxurious, practical and unexpected. Recent projects include a contemporary modernist estate in California, an English country manor house and a modern high rise pied à terre in NYC. Current work includes a duplex in NYC, the reception hall and conference room of an industrial companys' headquarters and the reconfiguration of a flat in London. Design philosophy: attention to detail and client needs are primary.

Jin Jian

Jin Jian. Zhu Ping Shang She, Hangzhou, China. Founded in 2009, ZPSS specialise in interior and furniture design. Recent projects include a villa in Hangzhou, the office building for Zhejiang TV station and a flagship store for Italian fashion brand DOXA. Current work includes a 10,000 sq m office building and a 1200 sq m private house. Design philosophy: art and design come from life and should serve for life.

Greg Natale

Greg Natale. Greg Natale Design, NSW, Australia. Integrating architecture, interior design and decoration. Recent work includes a variety of projects focused across Sydney, including a Palm Beach inspired home, a French inspired home in Bellevue Hill, the renovation of a Victorian terrace and an inner-city warehouse office space for a leading Australian fashion brand. Current projects include a sprawling county horse stud in Geelong, a grand new riverside home and guesthouse in Brisbane and a glamorous Sydney inner-city penthouse. Design philosophy: holistic.

Suzanne Lovell

Suzanne Lovell. Suzanne Lovell Inc, Chicago, USA. Luxury residential interior architecture, design and decoration with meticulous attention to detail. Current projects include a private owner's suite at the St. Regis, Manhattan, an historic renovation of a 7000 sq ft landmark Howard Van Doren Shaw penthouse in Chicago and a Manhattan penthouse in Trump World Tower. Recent projects include a penthouse in Chicago, the renovation and restoration of an iconic 1970's interior originally created by Arthur Elrod on Lake Shore Drive in Chicago, a San Francisco penthouse apartment and Carmel Beachfront Estate. Design philosophy: to create couture environments for extraordinary living.

Argent Design

Nicola Fontanella. Argent Design, London. A multi faceted international practice. The company provides a full turn-key design service for private residences and members clubs, aircraft and super yachts. Recent projects include a 9000 sq ft waterfront mansion in Miami, a luxury property development in Barbados, prestigious apartments in Monaco, New York and Hong Kong and several high end developments in London. Current work includes Amberwood House in Knightsbridge, a large mews house in Culross Street, a 20,000 sq ft Arts & Crafts residence in Bishop's Avenue, a lateral conversion of two apartments into one single residence and the restoration of a Robert Adam terrace. Design philosophy: 'we strive to provide exquisite design which is comfortable, elegant and unique.'

Yuna Megre

Yuna Megre, Megre Interiors, Moscow, Russia. A boutique practice founded in 2008, specialising in hospitality design internationally. Recent projects include Sixty/Sushi Baba, the highest restaurant in Europe with magnificent 360 degree views over Moscow, Mari Vanna

restaurant in a classic London townhouse and Don't Tell Mama, an opulent glam rock lounge bar in the heart of Moscow, awarded Best New Design by Time Out. Current work includes an apartment building on the prestigious Golden Mile, 50 St James, the transformation of an 18th century building into a new members club with 2 restaurants, bar, boutique hotel, spa, roof terrace and members lounges in London's St James and a luxury airport lounge for Mastercard elite clients set in Moscow's Sheremetievo Airport. Design philosophy: intuitive.

TaiMing Interior Design

Shu Yilan. TaiMing Interior Design, Shanghai, China. Commissions are high end, both commercial and residential throughout China and Singapore. Current projects include Jalan Sultan boutique hotel Singapore, Pudong Resort Hotel, Shanghai and Yuhuashan serviced apartments Shanghai. Design philosophy: to find the balance between real and ideal.

Julia Buckingham

Julia Buckingham Edelmann. Buckingham Interiors & Design, Chicago, USA. Current projects include a 17,000 square foot French provincial style home in Michigan, two condominiums in the Aqua building in Chicago's Lake Shore East neighbourhood and a second unit for a family in a condominium building on Chicago's Gold Coast. Recent work includes the complete renovation of an early 20th century Mediterranean style home in the historic Chicago suburb of Lake Forest, a mid-century home in Phoenix and a 19th century North Shore home.

Honky

Chris Dezille. Honky, London. A multi discipline architecture and interior design practice that provides a comprehensive service for private clients, property developers and hospitality sectors. Recent work includes the refurbishment of a townhouse, an extensive family residence and a lateral apartment. Current projects include an apartment building and a duplex penthouse in Central London, a boutique hotel in Montenegro and a major refurbishment of a substantial residence in Hampstead. Honky's philosophy: combine cutting edge detail with exceptional quality. We say: consistently at the top of their game.

Lev
Lugovskoy

Lev Lugovskoy. Midlife Crisis, Moscow, Russia. An individually run practice specialising in residential projects for private clients internationally. Recent work includes a series of country clubhouses in Khimki and an office space and private loft both in Moscow. Current work includes three private houses in Astana and an administrative residence for city government in Kazakhstan. Design philosophy: devoted to detail.

Anemone Wille Våge

Anemone Wille Våge. Anemone Wille Våge Interior Design, Oslo, Norway. Work is residential and commercial including hotels, restaurants, offices, homes and chalets. Current projects include Hotel Union Øye, restaurant Eik Annen Etage, restaurant Sawan and private residential projects. Recent work includes Hotel Post in Sweden, The Thief Hotel in Oslo, Highland Lodge at Geilo plus further private homes. Design philosophy: in harmony with architecture and surroundings.

Katharine Pooley

Katharine Pooley. Katharine Pooley Interior Design, London. One of London's most sought-after designers with commissions for landmark commercial and residential projects around the world. Recent work includes an extensive 4 bedroom private villa in Doha, a duplex apartment in The Lancasters and a 4500 sq ft late 18th century Tuscan farmhouse surrounded by olive groves in the hills of Chianti. Current projects include the reconfiguration of a 40,000 sq ft residential and commercial property, a 40,000 sq ft private family villa in Kuwait and a 3000 sq ft Katharine Pooley flagship store in Doha with KP own-label designs. Design philosophy: understated elegance.

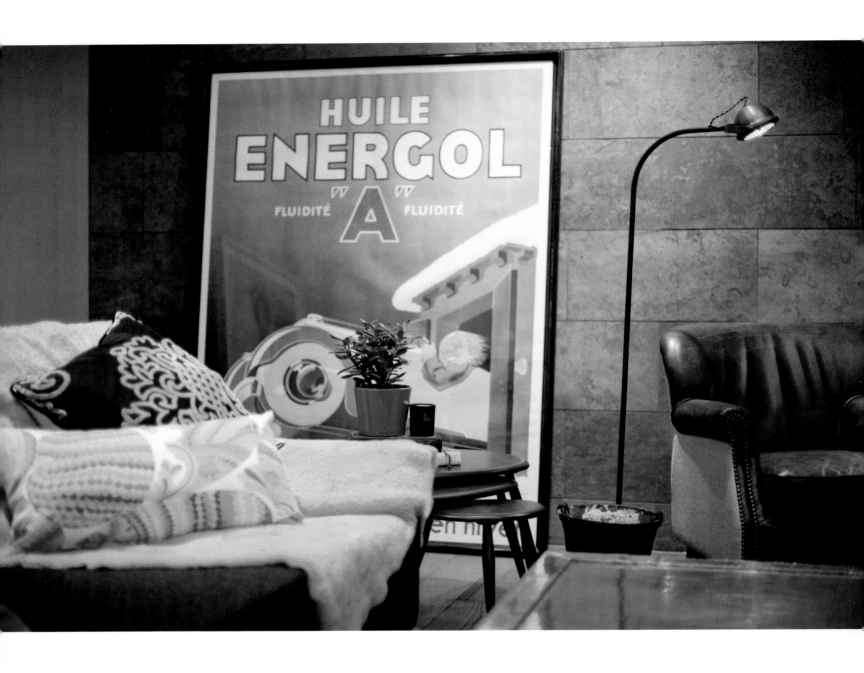

Matrushka

Joanna Berryman. Matrushka, London. Specialising in witty, rough-luxe designs with a personalised service. Recent projects include the transformation of an old East London photographic studio, the design and build of a pop-up Rum Shack installation within Floridita club, Soho and the redesign of an Edwardian mansion in Hampstead. Current work includes the refurbishment and restoration of a Glastonbury estate, the transformation of office space within the West Wing at Somerset House, London and the complete overhaul of a penthouse within a large Georgian building in Cavendish Square. Design philosophy: strength, style and comfort.

Zeynep Fadillioglu

Zeynep Fadillioglu. ZFD, Istanbul, Turkey. Established by Zeynep Fadillioglu in 1995, ZF Design specialises in a broad range of projects including luxurious residences, hotels, restaurants, product design, window design, set design and mosques for an international clientele. Zeynep's work is renowned for its rich colours, texture, textiles and patterns. Current works includes two mosques in Bahrain, an 800 sq m Bosphorus mansion in Istanbul, a 1500 sq m private villa in Jordan, an 1800 sq m villa in Oman and a 700 sq m house in Jeddah. Design philosophy: combine traditional with contemporary for universal appeal. We say: former winner of the AM Award, Zeynep is creating some of the world's greatest interiors.

Arent
& Pyke

Juliette Arent & Sarah-Jane Pyke. Arent & Pyke, Sydney, Australia. A boutique practice established in 2007. Arent & Pyke approach each project in response to the client, creating personal tailor made spaces. Commissions are high end and residential, with over forty projects across Sydney. The practice's first international commission was recently completed in New York.

A.M.P. Interiors

Aristos Migliaressis-Phocas. A.M.P. Interiors, London. Luxury design consultancy for an international clientele. Recent commissions include a private residence in Knightsbridge, a penthouse in the hills of Athens and a bachelor pad in Chelsea. Current projects include a penthouse in St John's Wood, a summerhouse on the coast of Athens and a pied à terre in Kensington. Design philosophy: reinvent the classic.

Jimmie Martin & McCoy

Jimmie Karlsson, Martin Nihlmar and Sally Anne McCoy. Jimmie Martin & McCoy, London. Specialising in luxury residences, nightclubs, restaurants and hotels. Current projects include a boutique hotel in Buckinghamshire, a Holland Park townhouse and a Hampstead penthouse. Recent work includes the warehouse conversion of a Swedish model agency, the Soho office of a hedgefund and a country pub. Design philosophy: luxury without rules.

Kit Kemp

Kit Kemp. Firmdale Hotels, London. Design director for Firmdale Hotels, comprising 8 hotels and 6 bars & restaurants in London and New York. Kit won the Andrew Martin International Designer of the Year Award in 2008. Recent projects include the Wool House exhibition in association with Campaign for Wool at Somerset House and Dorset Square Hotel. Current work includes Ham Yard Hotel due to open in London in June 2014, followed by another hotel in midtown New York in 2015. Design philosophy: hotels should be living things not stuffy institutions. We say: the world's best loved hotel designer.

Francisco Neves

Francisco Neves. 5 Janelas Design de Interiores, Guimarães, Portugal. Private and commercial work including houses, apartments, public spaces, bars, clubs and themed parties. Recent work includes a private house, a patisserie 'Pastelaria Fina' and an apartment each in Guimarães plus a holiday apartment on the North coast of Portugal. Ongoing projects include the company's new showroom in Guimarães and a beach house and country house. Design philosophy: inspired by music and travel Francisco creates each interior as if it were his last.

The Design Practice by UBER

Simon & Jim Evans and team. The Design Practice by Uber, Cheshire, UK. An award winning team. Recent projects include a Chairman's apartment for pre match gatherings, a contemporary golfing lodge overlooking Gleneagles fairway and the conversion of a farmhouse and outbuildings complete with 6000 sq ft underground leisure 'playground'. Current work includes a sympathetically modernised Georgian property, a Gibraltar development of 8 contemporary vertical glass super prime houses overlooking the harbour and a 35,000 sq ft classically styled new build in Cheshire.

Matthew Frederick. M. Frederick Interiors, NJ, USA. With offices in New York and Los Angeles, M. Frederick specialise in providing complete turn-key design solutions. Recent projects include the complete renovation of a 45,000 sq ft 19th century Italianate mansion in New Jersey, an 18th century residence in Krestovsky Island, St. Petersburg and an interiors concept for a 2200 sq ft three bedroom holiday residence in Nice, Cote d'Azur. Current work includes construction consulting for an Equestrian Estate, Ocala, Florida, a beach cottage in Provincetown, Massachusetts and the redesign and renovation of a 1200 sq ft mid town residence, New York. Design philosophy: elegant living for everyday life.

Matthew Frederick

Silvina Macipe Krontiras. SMK Interiors, Marousi, Greece. Founded in 2008, the company provides an architecture and interior design service for enduring turn-key projects. Recent work includes several villas including one on the seafront in the south west of Attica and an ethnic but contemporary style home in the south suburbs of Attica. Current projects include the redesign of a new restaurant and two seaside bars in a luxury resort hotel in an Aegean island plus a new seaside villa located in the Sporades islands. Design philosophy: homes are the reflection of who we are and what we believe.

SMK Interiors

The Gallery HBA
London

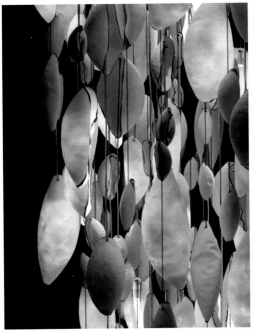

Inge Moore. The Gallery HBA, London. Bespoke interiors for the hospitality and residential sectors. Recent projects include the legendary Art Nouveau Hotel Maria Cristina, San Sebastian, Spain, a transformation of the Royal Suite at the InterContinental London Park Lane and the rustic yet refined interior of the hotel Alpina Gstaad, Switzerland. Current work includes a five star luxury hotel in Jerusalem, the design for Omkar 1973 Worli, a group of three exclusive residential towers in Mumbai and the contemporary refurbishment of The Westin Excelsior, Florence. Design philosophy: fusing tradition and innovation.

BRICKS

James van der Velden. BRICKS, Amsterdam, The Netherlands. After experience as a designer for Kelly Hoppen, James set up his own studio in 2010. Recent projects include the renovation of Keizersgracht loft, the styling of the hotel lobby and SocietyM meeting rooms at Citizen M Hotel London Bankside and a flat for a Dutch top model. Three current projects include the complete renovation of a 5 storey canal house and the styling of the hotel lobby & rooftop bar on the 19th floor of CitizenM New York Times Square. Bricks design philosophy is to create eclectic projects which translate a house into a home.

Helen
Green
Design

Natalia Miyar. Helen Green Design, London. Led by Natalia Miyar, Helen Green Design is a comprehensive studio which encompasses interior design, interior architecture and British made bespoke furniture, wallpapers and fabrics. Current work includes a townhouse in Belgravia and a country house in West Sussex. Recent projects include a hotel in Barbados, a country house in Hampshire and a town house in Pelham Crescent. Philosophy: design solutions which enhance homes and lives.

Turner
Pocock

Bunny Turner & Emma Pocock. Turner Pocock, London & Geneva. With experience in the commercial art world and property developing, they tailor the scope of each project to meet the precise requirements of the client. Recent work includes the complete reconfiguration of a Chelsea Mews house, the redesign and extension of a mid-terraced family house and the remodeling of a triplex apartment on a garden square including a dramatic glass bridge extension. They say: allow the brief and the architecture to create a clients perfect home. We say: rising stars.

493

4 Rose Uniacke
Rose Uniacke
76-82 Pimlico Road, London SW1X 8PL
Tel: +44 (0)207 730 7050
Fax: +44 (0)845 280 3290
mail@roseuniacke.com
www.roseuniacke.com

10 Jan des Bouvrie
Studio Jan des Bouvrie
Kooltjesbuurt 1, 1411 R2 Naarden
The Netherlands
Tel: +31 (0)35 699 6200, Fax: +31 (0)35 631 0100
l.vanpelt@jandesbouvrie.nl
www.jandesbouvrie.nl

16 John Loecke & Jason Oliver Nixon
Madcap Cottage
17 Chester Court, Brooklyn
New York 11225 USA
Tel: +1 917 513 9143
jason@madcapcottage.com
wwwmadcapcottage.com.

20 David Scott
David Scott Interiors Ltd
1123 Broadway
Suite 805 New York NY 10010 USA
Tel: +1 212 829 0703, Fax +1 212 829 0718
info@davidscottinteriors.com
www.davidscottinteriors.com

28 Hank M. Chao
Mohen Design International
Rm 301, No 18 Yu Hang Road
Yao Jiang Int'l Tower
Office Building 200080, Shanghai, China
Tel: +8621 338 71946
Fax: +8621 338 71940
mohen@mohen-design.com
www.mohen-design.com

32 Aleksandra Laska
Ola Laska
00-079 Warsaw, Poland
Ul. Krakowskie Przedmiescie 85m5
Tel: +48 609 522 942
Fax: +48 22 826 0796
aleksandra.laska@gmail.com

38 Catarina Rosas, Claudia Soares Pereira
& Catarina Soares Pereira
Casa do Passadico
Largo Sao Joao de Souto, 4700 Braga, Portugal
Tel: +351 253 619 988, Fax: +351 253 213 110
mail@casadopassadico.com
www.casadopassadico.com

42 Ana Cordeiro
Prego Sem Estopa
Calcada do Combro no 36
1200-114 Lisbon, Portugal
Tel: +351 213 421 583
Fax: +351 213 429 719
pregosemestopa@sapo.pt
www.pregosemestopa.pt

46 Kate Instone & Natascha Dartnall
Blush Design
Studio 6, Elysium Gate
126-128 New Kings Road, London SW6 4LZ
Tel: 0207 111 9792
design@blush-design.co.uk
www.blush-design.co.uk

50 Stefano Dorata
Stefano Dorata Architetto
00197 Roma, 12A/14 Via Antonio Bertoloni, Italy
Tel: +39 (0)6 80 84 747
Fax: +39 (0)6 80 77 695
studio@stefanodorata.com
www.stefanodorata.com

54 Kelly Hoppen
Kelly Hoppen Interiors
102a Chepstow Road
St Stephen's Yard, London W2 5QS
Tel: +44 (0)207 471 3350
Fax: +44 (0)207 727 6460
interiors@kellyhoppen.co.uk
www.kellyhoppenretail.com

60 Jennifer Jones
Jennifer Jones Interior Design
22 9th Avenue, Parktown North
2193, Gauteng, South Africa
Mobile: +27 82 883 0131
Fax: +27 86 760 5002
jen@jjid.co.za
www.jjid.co.za

66 Polina Belyakova, Ekaterina Grigorieva
& Ekaterina Ponyatovskaya
Suite Home Interiors
119048 Moscow, Usatcheva Str
2 Bld 3, App 166, Russia
Tel: +7985 970 5617
suitehome@gmail.com
www.suitehome.ru

70 Emma Sims-Hilditch
Sims Hilditch Limited
The Studio, West Kington, Wiltshire SN14 7JJ
Tel: +44 (0)1249 783 087
info@simshilditch.com
www.simshilditch.com

74 Staffan Tollgard
Staffan Tollgard Design Group
100 Westboune Studios
242 Acklam Road, London W10 5JJ
Tel: +44 (0)207 575 3185
Fax: +44 (0)207 575 3186
monique@tollgard.co.uk
www.tollgard.co.uk

80 Nikolay Lyashenko, Alexandr Tsimailo
& Olga Kolesnik
Tsimailo Lyashenko & Partners
22/1 Sadovaya Karetnaya, Moscow, Russia
Tel/Fax: +7 (495) 790 7976
info@tip-ab.ru
levanovich@tlp-ab.ru
www.tlp-ab.ru

84 Kiki Andreou
Kiki Andreou Interiors
5 Erythrou Stavrou 5
15123 Maroussi, Athens, Greece
Tel: +30 210 680 0431
Fax: +30 210 6801 527
kiki.andr@otenet.gr
www.kikiandreouinteriors.com

88 Birgitte Orne
Birgitta Orne Interior Design
Ostermalmsgatan 65, 114 50 Stockholm, Sweden
Tel: +46 708 279 888
info@birgittaorne.com
www.birgittaorne.com

92 Karen Howes
Taylor Howes Designs
29 Fernshaw Road, London SW10 OTG
Tel: +44 (0)207 349 9017
Fax: +44 (0)207 349 9018
admin@taylorhowes.co.uk
www.taylorhowes.co.uk

96 Li Bo
Cimax Design Engineering (Hong Kong) Ltd
7B Building 9, Haiying Changcheng
No 2 Wen Xin Road, ShenZhen
GuangDong, China
Tel/Fax: +86 0755 2644 8677
libodesign@126.com
www.libodesign.com

102 Carmo Aranha & Rosario Tello
Sa Aranha & Vasconcelos
Rua Vale Formoso no 45
1950 - 279 Lisbon, Portugal
Tel: +351 21 845 3070
Fax: +351 21 849 5325
info@saaranhavasconcelos.pt
www.saaranhavasconcelos.pt

108 Poppy & Charlotte O'Neil
Poco Designs
24 Glenmore Road
Paddington NSW 2021, Australia
Tel: +02 8356 9632
Fax: +02 9380 9486
poppy@pocodesigns.com.au
www.pocodesigns.com.au

112 John Beven & Richard Wilkinson
Wilkinson Beven Design Ltd
1a Main Street, Dickens Heath
Solihull, Birmingham B90 1UB
Tel: +44 (0)121 744 1458
Fax: +44 (0)121 744 0129
design@wilkinsonbevendesign.com
www.wilkinsonbevendesign.com

118 ShuHeng Huang
Sherwood Design, Room 2
17F, No 2, Lane 150, Sec 5, Sinyi Rd
Sinyi District, Taipei City 110 Taiwan
Tel: +886 02 663 657 88
Fax: +886 02 663 658 68
sh@sherwood-inc.com
www.sherwood-inc.com

122 Mark Rielly & Adam Court
Antoni Associates
4th Floor, 109 Hatfield Street, Gardens
Cape Town 8001, South Africa
Tel: +27 (0) 21 468 4400
Fax: +27 (0) 21 461 5408
info@aainteriors.co.za
www.aainteriors.co.za

128 Andrew Dunn & Alex Michelin
Finchatton
Jubilee House, 2 Jubilee Place, London SW3 3TQ
Tel: +44 (0)207 349 1120
info@finchatton.com
www.finchatton.com

134 Fabio Galeazzo
Galeazzo Design
Rua Antonio Bicudo, 83
Sao Paulo 05418 - 010, Brazil
Tel: +55 11 3064 5306
galeazzo@fabiogaleazzo.com.br
www.fabiagaleazzo.com.br

140 Chou Yi
JOY-CHOU Yi Interior Design Studio
No. 204, Sec 1, Wucuan Wu. Road
West Dist, Taizhong City, 403, Taiwan
Tel: +886 4 2375 9455
Fax: +886 4 2376 3623
joyis.chou@msa.hinet.net
www.joychou.com

144 Scott Sanders
Scott Sanders LLC
27 West 24th St. Suite 803
New York NY 10010 USA
Tel: +212 343 8298
Fax: +212 343 8299
info@scottsandersllc.com
www.scottsandersllc.com

148 Nikki Hunt
Design Intervention
75E Loewen Road, Tanglin Village
Singapore 248845
Tel: +(65) 6506 0920
Fax: +(65) 6486 7418
info@diid.sg
www.designintervention.com.sg

152 Pamela Makin
Les Interieurs
176 Barrenjoey Road
Newport, NSW 2106 Australia
Tel: +0408 500 400
pamela@lesinterieurs.com.au
www.lesinterieurs.com.au

156 Enrica Fiorentini Delpani
Studio Giardino
Via Caselle 6, 25125 Brescia, Italy
Tel: +39 030 353 2548
studiogiardino55@libero.it
www.studiogiardino.eu

160 Elliot March & James White
March and White Architecture
and Interior Design
103 Charing Cross Road
London WC2H 0DT
Tel: 0207 240 3464
info@marchandwhite.com
www.marchandwhite.com

164 Roy Teo
Kri:eit Associates Pte Ltd
Suite 3-3 @ The Mill
5 Jalan Kilang, Singapore 159405
Tel: +65 6733 0330
Fax: +65 6733 0440
interiors@krieit.com
www.krieit.com

168 Lucia Valzelli
Dimore Di Lucia Valzelli
Via Gramsci No 18, 25121 Brescia, Italy
Tel: +39 (0) 30 280 274
Fax: +39 (0) 30 280 274
info@dimorestudio.com
www.dimorestudio.com

174 Louis H. Buhrmann
Louis Henri Ltd
Penthouse 4, Hewlett House
Havelock Terrace, London SW8 4AS
Tel: +44 (0)207 622 8343
Fax: +44 (0)207 498 7261
louis@louishenri.com
www.louishenri.com

178 Jordi Vayreda
Jordivayredaprojectteam
Montsalvatge
32-17800 Olot (Catalonia), Spain
Tel: +34 972 27 18 49
jordi@jordivayreda.com
www.jordivayreda.com

182 Jenny Weiss & Helen Bygraves
Hill House Interiors
1st Floor, 32-34 Baker Street
Weybridge, Surrey KT13 8AT
jenny@hillhouseinteriors.com
helen@hillhouseinteriors.com
www.hillhouseinteriors.com

186 Danny Cheng Ping Kwan
Dang Cheng Interiors Ltd
14/F Caltex House, 258 Hennessy Road
Wan Chai, Hong Kong
Tel: (852) 2877 3282
Fax: (852) 2877 3299
info@dannycheng.com.hk
www.dannycheng.com.hk

190 Sera Hersham Loftus
Sera of London
6 Alma Square
London NW8 9QW
Tel: 07977 534 115
sera@seraoflondon.com
www.seraoflondon.com

194 Jorge Canete
Jorge Canete Interior Design Philosophy,
Chateau de Saint-Saphorin-sur-Morges
Le Pave 2
CH - 1113 Saint-Saphorin-sur-Morges (VD),
Switzerland
Tel: +41 78 710 25 34
Fax: +41 21 944 37 57
info@jorgecanete.com
www.jorgecanete.com

198 Holger Kaus
Holger Kaus
Gugghof, Hofwies 50
83714 Miesbach
Germany
Tel: +49 8025 / 99 74 60
Fax: +49 8025 / 99 74 629
g.ludwig@holgerkaus.com
www.holgerkaus.com

202 Irina Glik
Geometry Design
45 Kutuzovsky Prospect
Moscow 121170
Russia
Tel/Fax: +7 495 771 7041
geometry-moscow@mail.ru
www.geometry-moscow.ru

206 Jim Gauthier & Susan Stacy
Gauthier-Stacy Inc
112 Shawmut Avenue
6th Floor
Boston MA 02118 USA
kate@gauthierstacy.com
www.gauthierstacy.com

212 Chang Ching - Ping
Tien Fun Interior Planning Co Ltd
12F No 211 Chung Min Road, North District
Taichung City 404, Taiwan (ROC)
Tel: +886 4 220 18908
Fax: +886 4 220 36910
tf@mail.tienfun.com.tw
www.tienfun.com.tw

218 Law Ling Kit & Virginia Lung
One Plus Partnership Ltd
9/F New Wing
101 King's Road
North Point, Hong Kong
Tel: +852 2591 9308
Fax: +852 2591 9362
admin@onepluspartnership.com
www.onepluspartnership.com

222 Mr Mayank Gupta (Director)
Apartment 9, Design Studio N9
N-Block Market
Greater Kailash - 1
New Delhi 110048, India
Tel: +91 011 324 382 24/5
info@apartment9.in
www.apartment9.in

226 Paul Hecker & Hamish Guthrie
Hecker Guthrie
1 Balmain Street, Richmond
Victoria 3121 Australia
Tel: +61 3 9421 1644
Fax: +61 3 9421 1677
studio@heckerguthrie.com
www.heckerguthrie.com

230 Krista Hartmann
Krista Hartmann Interior AS
Kristinelundveien 6
0268 Oslo, Norway
Tel: +47 970 64 654
krista@krista.no
www.krista.no

234 Thong Lei & Anne Noordam
Decoration Empire
Meridiaan 57-63, 2801 DA Gouda
The Netherlands
Tel: +31 182 58 3341
Fax: +31 182 583 351
info@decorationempire.nl
www.decorationempire.nl

240 Daniel Kostiuc
Intarya Ltd
8 Albion Riverside
8 Hester Road
London SW11 4AX
Tel: +44 (0)207 349 8020
Fax: +44 (0)207 349 8001
info@intarya.com
www.intarya.com

246 Yasumichi Morita
Glamorous Co Ltd
2F 2-7-25 Motoazabu, Minato-Ku
Tokyo 106-0046 Japan
Tel: +81 3 5475 1037
Fax: +81 3 5475 1038
info@glamorous.co.jp
www.glamorous.co.jp

252 Roy Azar
Roy Azar Architects
Prado Norte 125 - PB
Lomas de Chapultepec
Mexico D.F. 11000
Tel/Fax: +(52) 55 5520 9060
ra@royazararchitects.com
www.royazararchitects.com

258 Nick Candy
Candy & Candy
Rutland House, Rutland Gardens
Knightsbridge, London SW7 1BX
Tel: +44 (0)207 590 1900
Fax: +44 (0)207 590 1901
info@candyandcandy.com
www.candyandcandy.com

264 Bin Wu
Hong Kong W.Architectural Design Co. Ltd
1298, Huaihaizhong Road, Shanghai, China
Tel: +86 (21) 3423 0218
Fax: +86 (21) 5407 7476
wubin516@hotmail.com
www.wdesign.hk

268 Meryl Hare
Hare + Klein Interior Design
Level 1, 91 Bourke Street
Woolloomooloo
NSW 2011 Australia
Tel: +612 9368 1234
Fax: +612 9368 1020
info@hareklein.com.au
www.hareklein.com.au

274 Cheng Si-Leung Ivan
Ivan C Design Limited
Flat 1, 13/F Block A
Gold Way Industrial Centre
16-20 Wing Kin Road, Kwai Chung
New Territories, Hong Kong
Tel: +852 987 37703
Fax: +852 255 62023
icdl20111@live.com
www.icdl-hk.com

278 Stephan Menn
Menn Architekt
Wittlaerer Kamp 1
40489 Dusseldorf, Germany
Tel: + 49 172 213 0544
mennarchitekt@vodafone.de
www.menn.de
www.fausel-biskamp.de

282 Federica Palacios
Federica Palacios Design
3 Cour St-Pierre 1204 Geneva
Switzerland
Tel: +41 22 310 22 76
Fax: +41 22 310 22 86
andreane@federicapalaciosdesign.com
www.federicapalaciosdesign.com

286 Alan Chan
Alan Chan Design Company
1901 Harcourt House
39 Gloucester Road
Wanchai, Hong Kong
acdesign@alanchandesign.com
www.alanchandesign.com

292 Helene Forbes Hennie
Christian's & Hennie
Skovveien 6
N 0257 Oslo, Norway
Tel: +47 22 12 13 50
Fax: +47 22 12 13 51
info@christiansoghennie.no
www.christiansoghennie.no

298 Hasan Çalislar & Kerem Erginoglu
Erginoglu & Calislar Architects
Sair Necati Sok, No 14
Ortakoy 34347
Istanbul, Turkey
Tel: +90 212 310 82 75
Fax: +90 212 260 98 85
ecmim@ecarch.com
www.ecarch.com

304 Nihal Zaki
Nihal Zaki Interiors
3 Ahmed Orabi St. Mohandessin
Cairo (12411) Egypt
Tel: + 201 0088 90900
Fax: + 202 334 78074
nsinteriors@yahoo.com
www.nihalzaki.com

310 Madina Vykhodtseva
Spark Décor
no 53a/2, Krasnoznamennaya Street
Ilyinsky Settlement
140121 Ramenskoe District
Moscow, Russia
sparkdecoration@gmail.com
mvdecor@mail.ru

314 Angelos Angelopoulos
Angelos Angelopoulos
5 Proairesiou Str 116 36 Athens, Greece
Tel/Fax: +30 210 756 7191
design@angelosangelopoulos.com
www.angelosangelopoulos.com

318 Elin Fossland
Elin Fossland Interiorarkitekt
Kirkegata 8, 3016 Drammen, Norway
& PO BOX 275, Bragernes
3001 Drammen, Norway
Tel: +916 64684
elin@arkitektfossland.no
www.arkitektfossland.no

322 Ken Freivokh
Ken Freivokh Design
Universal Marina, Crableck Lane
Sarisbury Green, Hampshire, SO31 7ZN
Tel: +44 (01) 1489 580 740
Fax: +44 (0) 1489 881 634
all@freivokh.com
www.freivokh.com

326 Kathleen Hay
Kathleen Hay Designs
PO Box 801
Nantucket MA 02554 USA
Tel: +508 228 1219
Fax: +508 228 6366
info@kathleenhaydesigns.com
www.kathleenhaydesigns.com

334 Atsuhiko Sugiyama
The Wholedesign Inc
Combo House,
2-12-5 Mita Meguro-ku 153-0062
Tokyo, Japan
Tel: +03 6303 1360
Fax: +03 6303 1361
tokyobranch@thewholedesign.com
www.thewholedesign.com

338 Martyn Lawrence Bullard
Martyn Lawrence Bullard Design
8550 Melrose Avenue
Los Angeles, CA 90069 USA
Tel: +323 655 5080
Fax: +323 655 5090
info@martynlawrencebullard.com
www.martynlawrencebullard.com

344 Tsung-Jen Lin
Crox International Co
No 15 Alley 395
Yuyuan Road, Jingan District
Shanghai, China 200040
Tel: +86 21 5230 3066
crox@crox.com.tw
www.crox.com.tw

350 Hugh Leslie
Hugh Leslie Design LLP
29 Thurloe Street, London SW7 2LQ
Tel: +44 (0)207 584 7185
Fax: +44 (0)207 581 7666
mail@hughleslie.com
www.hughleslie.com

354 Linda Steen
AS Scenario Interiorarkitekter MNL
Pilestredt 75C 0350 Oslo, Norway
Tel: +47 22 93 1250
nh@scenario.no
www.scenario.no

358 Steve Leung
Steve Leung Designers
30 /F Manhattan Place
23 Wang Tai Road
Kowloon Bay, Hong Kong
Tel: +852 2527 1600
Fax: +852 3549 8398
sld@steveleung.com
www.steveleung.com

362 Rachel Laxer
Rachel Laxer Interiors
48 Marlborough Place, London NW8 OPL
Tel: +44 (0)207 624 0728
info@rlaxerinteriors.com
www.rlaxerinteriors.com

366 Jin Jian
Zhu Ping Shang She
Floor 4, Xinshidai no 808 Gudun Road,
Hangzhou, China
Tel/Fax: +86 (571) 8894 9785
834237702@qq.com

372 Greg Natale
Greg Natale Design
Studio 6 Level 3
35 Buckingham Street
Surry Hills NSW 2010
Australia
Tel: +612 8399 2103
Fax: +612 8399 3104
info@gregnatale.com
www.gregnatale.com

378 Suzanne Lovell
Suzanne Lovell, Inc
225 West Ohio Street
Chicago Il 60654 USA
Tel: +312 595 1980
Fax: +312 595 9295
contact@suzannelovellinc.com
www.suzannelovellinc.com

382 Nicola Fontanella
Argent Design Limited
100 George Street
London W1U 8NU
Tel: +44 (0)207 563 4250
Fax: +44 (0)207 563 4251
office@argentdesign.co.uk
www.argentdesign.co.uk

388 Yuna Megre & Maria Elfimova
Megre Interiors
Bolshaya, Bronnaya St 7, Office 1
Moscow, Russia 123104
Tel/Fax: +7 (495) 690 5437
info@megreinteriors.com
www.megreinteriors.com

394 Shu Yilan
Taiming Interior Design (Shanghai) Co Ltd
Room 2701 Building B, Public Financial Center
No. 1023 West Yan'an Road
Shanghai 200050, China
Tel: +86 21611 30785
Fax: +86 21511 96868
syl@cn-tmi.com
www.cn-tmi.com

398 Julia Buckingham
Buckingham Interiors & Design Ltd
1820 West Grand Avenue
Chicago Il 60622, USA
Tel: +312 243 9975
Fax: +312 243 9978
info@buckinghamid.com
www.buckinghamid.com

404 Christopher Dezille
Honky
Unit 1 Pavement Studios
40-48 Bromells Road
London SW4 OBG
Tel: +44 (0)207 622 7144
Fax: +44 (0)207 622 7155
info@honky.co.uk
www.honky.co.uk

410 Lev Lugovskoy
Midlife Crisis
Mytischi, Sharapovskaya 1/3, 81
Moscow, Russia 141002
Tel: +7 985 273 6320
Fax: +7 495 505 7542
leoluggio@gmail.com
www.levlugovskoy.ru

414 Anemone Wille Vage
Wille Interior AS
Bygdoy Alle 58B
0265 Oslo, Norway
Tel: +47 22 55 32 00
anemone@anemone.no
www.anemone.no

418 Katharine Pooley
Katharine Pooley Ltd
160 Walton Street
London SW3 2JL
Tel: +44 (0)207 584 3223
Tel: +44 (0)207 584 5226
enquiries@katharinepooley.com
www.katharinepooley.com

422 Joanna Berryman
Matrushka
4 Willoughby Road
London NW3 1SA
Tel: +44 (0)207 435 1386
info@matrushka.co.uk
www.matrushka.co.uk

426 Zeynep Fadillioglu
Zeynep Fadillioglu Design
Ahmet Adnan Saygun Cad. Koru Sokak
Ulus Blok No2 Sitesi 1
Daire 3 Ulus, Istanbul, Turkey
Tel: +90 (212) 287 0936
Fax: +90 (212) 287 0994
design@zfdesign.com
www.zfdesign.com

430 Juliette Arent & Sarah - Jane Pyke
Arent & Pyke Pty Ltd
Studio3/36 Bayswater Road
Potts Point NSW 2011, Australia
Tel: +61 2 9 331 2802
Fax: +61 2 9 356 3673
design@arentpyke.com
www.arentpyke.com

434 Aristos Migliaressis - Phocas
A.M.P. Interiors
20 Bramham Gardens
London SW5 OJE
Tel: +44 (0)207 460 2091
info@amp-interiors.com
www.amp-interiors.com

438 Jimmie Karlsson, Martin Nihlmar,
Sally Anne McCoy
Jimmie Martin & McCoy
77 Kensington Church Street
London W8 4BG
Tel: +44 (0)207 93 777 85
contact@jimmiemartinandmccoy.com
www.jimmiemartinandmccoy.com

442 Kit Kemp
Firmdale Hotels
Head Office, 21 Golden Square
London W1F 9JN
Tel: +44 (0)207 581 4045
Fax: +44 (0)207 581 1867
reception@firmdale.com
www.firmdalehotels.com

448 Francisco Neves
5 Janelas Decoracao de Interiors
Rua Teixeira de Pascoais 40B
4800 - 073 Guimaraes, Portugal
Tel: +351 253 516 155
5janelas@gmail.com
www.5janelas.com

452 Simon & Jim Evans and Team
The Design Practice by UBER
Chelford Road
Ollerton, Knutsford
Cheshire WA16 8SB
Tel: +44 (0)8450 773 280
info@thedesignpractice.com
www.thedesignpractice.com

458 Matthew Frederick
M. Frederick LLC
49 Route 202, Far Hills
New Jersey 07931, USA
Tel: +908 669 4784
info@mfrederick.com
www.mfrederick.com

464 Silvina Macipe Krontiras
SMK Interiors
5 Lagadion Str
Marousi 15125, Athens, Greece
Tel: +30 210 8171 000
Fax: +30 210 8171 045
sm@smkinteriors.com
www.smkinteriors.com

470 Inge Moore
HBA London
The Gallery, 26 Westbourne Grove
London W2 5RH
Tel: +44 (0)207 313 3200
Fax: +44 (0)207 313 3239
london@hbadesign.com
www.hbadesign.com

478 James van der Velden
BRICKS Amsterdam
Maarten Jansz, Kosterstraat 18
1017 VZ Amsterdam
The Netherlands
Tel: +31 (0)6 2120 1272
info@bricks-amsterdam.com
www.bricksamsterdam.com

482 Natalia Miyar
Helen Green Design
29 Milner Street
London SW3 2QD
Tel: +44 (0)207 352 3344
Fax: +44 (0)207 352 5544
mail@helengreendesign.com
www.helengreendesign.com

488 Emma Pocock & Bunny Turner
Turner Pocock
204 Latimer Road, Kensington
London W10 6QY
Tel: +44 (0)203 463 2390
Tel: +44 (0)7798 533 363
info@turnerpocock.co.uk
www.turnerpocock.co.uk
and
Turner Pocock
3, Route de Geneve
1260 Nyon, Switzerland
Tel: +41 (0)7919 27558

© 2013 Andrew Martin International

Editor Martin Waller
Project Executive Annika Bowman
Design by Graphicom Design

Production by Nele Jansen, teNeues Verlag
Editorial coordination by Inga Wortmann, teNeues Verlag
Colour separation by SPM Print

teNeues Publishing Group
Kempen
Berlin
Cologne
Düsseldorf
Hamburg
London
Munich
New York
Paris

First published in 2013 by teNeues Verlag GmbH + Co. KG, Kempen

teNeues Verlag GmbH + Co. KG
Am Selder 37, 47906 Kempen, Germany
Phone: +49-(0)2152-916-0
Fax: +49-(0)2152-916-111
e-mail: books@teneues.de

Press department: Andrea Rehn
Phone: +49-(0)2152-916-202
e-mail: arehn@teneues.de

teNeues Digital Media GmbH
Kohlfurter Straße 41–43, 10999 Berlin, Germany
Phone: +49-(0)30-7007765-0

teNeues Publishing Company
7 West 18th Street, New York, NY 10011, USA
Phone: +1-212-627-9090
Fax: +1-212-627-9511

teNeues Publishing UK Ltd.
12 Ferndene Road, London, SE24 0AQ, UK
Phone: +44-(0)20-3542-8997

teNeues France S.A.R.L
39, rue des Billets, 18250 Henrichemont, France
Phone: +33-(0)2-4826-9348
Fax: +33-(0)1-7072-3482

www.teneues.com

Andrew Martin trade edition: ISBN 978-0-9558938-5-8-(A.M V.17)
teNeues trade edition: ISBN 978-3-8327-9723-2
Library of Congress Control Number: 2013940488
Printed in Italy

Bibliographic information published by the Deutsche Nationalbibliothek.
The Deutsche Nationalbibliothek lists this publication in the Deutsche Nationalbibliografie; detailed bibliographic data are available in
the Internet at http://dnb.d-nb.de.

Acknowledgments

The author and publisher wish to thank all the owners and designers of the projects featured in this book.

They also thank the following photographers:

Bo des Bouvrie, John Bessler, Antoine Bootz, Maoder Chou, Hanna Dlugosz, Michal Glinicki, Aleksandra Laska, Pawel Zak,
Francisco Almeida Dias, Pedro Ferreira, Francisco de Almeida Dias, Sebastian Nicholas, Giorgio Baroni, Mel Yates,
Elsa Young, William Webster, Simon McBride, Richard Gooding, Daniella Cesarei, Manolo Yllera, Natalia Tsoukala,
Anne Nyblaeus, David Garcia, Jon Day, Tom Sullam, Guojian Xie, Carlos de Vasconcellos, Pedro Ferreira,
Montse Garriga Grau, Anson Smart, Marc Berenguer, Dan Christaldi, Mike Toy, David Withycombe, Will Pryce, Black Wang,
Adam Letch, Tom Sullam, Richard Waite, Brian Van Den Brink, Celia Weiss, Maira Acayaba. Lufe Gomes, Lou Kwou-Chi,
Josh Klein, James Bleecker, Jo Ann Gamelo-Bernabe, Michele Biancucci, Umberto Favretto, Kilian O'Sullivan, Elisa Venturelli,
Aurora Zanetti, Giorgio Baroni, Richard Waite, Sergi Farres Perarnau, Raul Candales Franch, Thierry Cardineau,
Danny Cheng Interiors, Gisela Torres, Celine Michel, Marie de Goumoens, Christine Bauer, Svdijian Milinkovic,
Vladimir Klesov, Elena Koldunova, Sam Gray, Liu, Chun-Chieh, Jonathan Leijonhufvud, Ajax Law, Virginia Lung,
Mr. Hemant J, Khendilwal, Shannon Mc Grath, Ragnar Hartvig, Yvonne Wilhelmsen, Thong Lei, Seiryo Studio, I. Susa,
Edgardo Contreras, Candy & Candy, Bin Wu, Jenni Hare, Nicholas Watt, Zhi Kang, Yun Wei, Ying Hanghua,
Guido Havemann, Gilles Trillard, Mr. Alvin Chan, Stian Broch, Cemal Emden, Nihal Zaki Interiors, Sergey Ananiev,
Vangelis Paterakis, Mona Gundersen, Drew Kelly, Ken Freivokh, Jeffrey Allen Photography, Nakasa + Partners, Ave Studio,
Deborah Anderson, Tim Street Porter, Ji-Shou Wang, Wei-Hung Li, Shen Qiang, Mark Weeks Photography, Joe Condron,
Andreas von Einsiedel, Marcus Peel Photography, Gatis Rozenfelds, Ulso Tsang, Chen Zhong, Matthew Millman,
Adrian Briscoe, Shivi Isman, Jo Pawels, Gwen Shabka, Hang Mingchi, Anson Smart, Tony Soluri, Argent Design Limited,
Michael Stepanov, Dajun He, Eric Hausman, Peter Bennett, Patrick Steel, Leonid Chernous, Louise Billgert, Krister Engstrom,
Ray Main, Darren Chung, Julian Abrams, Simon Williams, Benno Thoma, Anson Smart, Tom Ferguson, Damian Russell,
Joseph Sinclair, Phil Matthews, Simon Brown, Miguel Angelo Carvalho de Oliveira, Bruno Barbosa, Karl Hopkins,
Peter Corcoran, John Bessler, Mr Paterakis, Mr Tempos, Jason Lang, Tim Beddow, Will Pryce, Ken Hayden,
Starwood Hotels & Resorts, Eric Laignel, Reto Guntli, Barbara de Hosson, Ray Main, Tom Sullam, Simon Brown,
Darren Chung, Tim Edwards, Sasha Gusov, Will Clarkson, Sean Myers.